PERSECUTED
FOR RIGHTEOUSNESS SAKE

Daniel M. Hayes, Sr.

PERSECUTED FOR RIGHTEOUSNESS SAKE

Copyright © 2014

All rights reserved.

ISBN# 9781 499578652

Table of Contents

Gratitude

First and foremost, I give all thanks to the Lord my God, for all the gifts, blessings
and accomplishments in my life.

To my special, loving and supportive family, my wife Janice and my children,
Danielle, Daniel Jr. and Danicia;

To my sisters, Shiela Hayes Greer and Angela Hayes Berry, and my brothers, Millard Hayes, Jr. and Johnny Hayes, for always being there for me;

To my church family, John Wesley United Methodist Church, Nashville, Tenn.

Dedicated to the memory of my parents Millard Hayes, Sr. and Violet E. Hayes, for their guidance and unconditional love; and

To the memory of my brothers,
GeAuthor and Joseph Hayes.

Acknowledgements

A special thanks to my editor, Celinda J. Hughes, and to those who have motivated me and continue to give me inspiration and encouragement for the journey.

Introduction

This book of stories and sermons is written to give strength, courage and the will to stand up and face the many trials that life can and will present and surprise us with.

Regardless of who we are, our status, our prominence, our position in the community, and even the church can change instantly and without warning. At a moment's notice life can throw you a curve like no one else can. It will remind you over and over that the Devil's attacks on God's people are true. They are consistent and just seem to keep coming. Every time you think you have conquered one problem, others arise. Every time you past one pack of trouble, more seems to show up. Every time you raise your head up and show that big smile, the woes of life immediately start wiping it away, and gently your head begins to lower itself again. There you are, looking, acting and feeling defeated. There you are throwing yourself a pity party, looking down, frowning on others, wishing them a fate similar to the one you are dealing with. You know how it is. Hate for everything and everybody starts to take over your being. You even come to the point where you feel lost, alone, beaten and down for the count. And, while this is going on, the Devil and his imps are rejoicing, "high-fiving" each other and saying, "We have done it again. We've completed another chapter in our victory book."

Oh, did I forget to tell you the job description of the Devil? According to St. John 10:10, the Devil's job is to kill, steal and destroy you. Who? You! Yes, Satan wants to kill, steal and destroy your motivation to do and become all that you can, and reach the heights that God expects you to reach. He wants to snatch your dreams and keep them from being realized. He wants to destroy your faith and belief in God. If you allow your past problems and your hang-ups, to hem up your dreams, you are only allowing the Devil and the world to defeat you. Remember this equation—if you have no vision, no forward progress and no dreams, you will never claim the prize that God has waiting for you, which means no victory.

When you spend all of your time working for the Lord, giving to the Lord, praising the Lord, lifting him up every chance you get, going out of your way to help those in need, and loving those deemed unlovable, your life can seem in a state of confusion. When you embrace those who claim to be your partners in the faith and ministry, only to have Satan and his partners try and take away all you have done and ever plan to accomplish, for the glory of God, your life goes off the path and the negativity begins to conflict with who you are. However, the one thing you cannot do is give in or allow the spirit of goodness and love that God has so graciously bestowed upon you the opportunity to be crushed.

This is the time when you must stand up for the Lord and show him who you are and whose you are. You must be ready to seize the victory that God wants you to have at all costs.

In other words, run until you feel all strength, power and energy are depleted. Even then, pray that God will grant you more so you can continue to move forward. God expects his faithful children to keep going forward. Never stop! Never quit!

Your forward progress indicates that you trust the Almighty to see you through every trial and temptation. It means you truly believe God is all powerful and knowing. It further says that you are faithfully standing on his word and his promises, and you are ready to shine as the fruit of God's labors.

Giving up and throwing in the towel is unacceptable. It is an indication that you are a quitter. Not only are you quitting on yourself, you are quitting on God. It means you believe that God has neither the strength nor the power to deliver you, or to be there for you when you need him the most. Forward progress is an action that screams, YES Lord, I believe, I trust and I know the prize is mine for the taking!"

Now is the time for those who truly believe in and know the Lord to do more than just talk, but to live and walk as if powered by faith, with the knowledge that God will help you secure the victory.

I challenge you as you read this collection of stories and sermons that you evaluate yourself, your life and your faith, as you continue to walk with the Lord.

Psalm 54:4 says, "But surely, God is my helper; the Lord is the upholder of my life." In other words, God will lift you up during the times that your strength fails.

- He will protect you from all manner of danger.
- He will fight for you as a mighty battle axe.
- He puts himself in harm's way for us.

Our gratitude and thanksgiving can be demonstrated by remaining steadfast, and not tiring or turning our backs on God.

> The prophet Isaiah says in 40:27-31,
> [27] "Why do you say, O Jacob, and complain,
> O Israel, "My way is hidden from the LORD;
> my cause is disregarded by my God"?
> [28] Do you not know? Have you not heard?
> The LORD is the everlasting God,
> the Creator of the ends of the earth.
> He will not grow tired or weary,
> and his understanding no one can
> fathom. [29] He gives strength to the weary and
> increases the power of the weak.
> [30] Even youths grow tired and weary, and young
> men stumble and fall;

[31] but those who hope in the LORD will renew their strength.
They will soar on wings like eagles;
They will run and not grow weary,
They will walk and not be faint."

Understand that through your faith, God will grant you power to change your situation, regardless of how challenges come upon you. Your enemies cannot stop you. The world and all of its challenges cannot prevent you from going forward. If you are not standing up for God all the time, others will try their best to bring you down. Look at what they did to Jesus. He was persecuted for righteousness sake, for doing good, helping those in need and raising up the bowed down heads of those who were lost. He was scoffed and beaten for easing troubled minds, mending broken hearts and drying tear-filled eyes, with assurance of a brighter day. He was humiliated for helping the lost find their way; for feeding the hungry, healing the sick and standing up for the weak. He was mocked and derided for giving hope to the hopeless and for encouraging the shamed and outcast that they were still loved by a God who would never leave or forsake them. This holy, majestic, Messiah, was disregarded and discarded. If they did it to Jesus, why would you believe that people of this world would not betray, turn away and leave you stranded and alone? Who do you think you are to go unscathed by the vicious wrath of humankind? If they persecuted Jesus, surely, we can be ready to bear our crosses, take our licks, be called what we are not and even thrown under the bus by those we call family and friends.

But, as Jesus stood the test, never stopped, never gave up and never stopped being the Lord of our lives, so we must prevail, keep fighting, keep praising, keep giving and keep believing that our blessings, our resurrection and our total victory will come. Yes, it will if we mount up on the wings of a mighty eagle and fly over our troubles, faults, failures, mistakes, injustices and all that tries to stop, hinder and destroy us. We must believe with confidence that we cannot and will not be taken off the course of God's goodness towards us.

It is my prayer that you are renewed in your commitment to God, and that you regain a faith that will take you beyond anything you could ever imagine for your life.

You will be able not only to claim your faith in God, you will walk and live it fully and completely. You will soar above the worst and experience the best. O, Taste, see and learn it is possible to rebuild your faith in God.

Through these messages of hope and inspiration revealed by God, you will be able to let the eagle in you come out. When that happens, get ready to fly!

The Power: Building, Walking, Living Your Faith

Part I - Building Your Faith

Life brings with it many challenges that can devastate you, rip your positive momentum apart and leave you helpless, hopeless and even divided within. Things can happen in your life that seem simple and not too important, but can have a tragic effect on your life.

One lie told on you or someone you love can disrupt your existence and cause you to lose respect, reputation, position in your company and your community. It can seem like "death". This "death" can send you reeling so much that the spinning never seems to stop. As a result you can grieve for years, leaving you in a dark place, not knowing or understanding how, when or if you will ever be restored to the person you once were. The pain is unbearable with no relief in sight.

The strife that rips through your life creates a chasm that becomes so deep everything you once called normal is an upside down switch in reality. You may even think you have stumbled into another dimension in some other world, where your financial hardships send you off the deep end and hope for a brighter day is a far-in-the-distance glimpse of what could be. In this altered state of existence, your life is reshaped, dreams are diminished and your outlook and direction for a better life gets washed away by the overwhelming waves of your own cynicism.

As you experience this formidable "death", the status of important relationships can change and be truly devastating. You have never experienced the kind of brokenness from the heart to your very soul. It can leave you feeling that life is not worth living. That level of bitterness conquers you in the most profound way. Rejection from the one you love and care about makes you feel as though you are on a deserted island—lost, alone and forgotten—especially when it is not your choice. When the outpouring of your heart for the love of your life is returned with rejection and deceit, only a hollow shell remains, and, again, the grief is unlike no other emotion you have ever felt.

Betrayal of family and friends can result from this manufactured life, and becomes another of the hardest things to cope with. Those you have loved, cared for, protected, stood up for, shared with, and gone out of your way to help simply disappear. In this alternate existence you find betrayal is your reality, as you try and recover from viciously, maliciously and repetitively being stabbed in the back.

To overcome these traumatic experiences, you must have strong, unwavering faith in God. Therefore, each day of your life you must work to rebuild your faith in God. Faith-building must take place before you can live or walk your faith. It must take place so you can have solid footing to travel your journey. Strong faith can and will sustain you during trying times. It will pick you up after you have been knocked down and torn into innumerable pieces.

- Your faith is your solid foundation, and the key to living a positive and rewarding life.
- Your faith is your assurance of overcoming any hardships that the alternate life of betrayal and "death" presents you.
- Your faith will lead you back from bitter defeats and restore your reality to a state better than it was before.

True faith will turn your life around, even when everyone else has given up on you, and told you you're fighting a lost cause. Restoration begins when you focus on building your faith in God. Then and only then will you be able to handle the blows of life that will surely come.

The Bible tells us in Romans 10:17 that, "Faith comes by hearing and by hearing the word of God." In other words, it is hard to build faith without the word of God. If you want to build your life on something solid, that won't give way, won't bend or break, won't fail, even when your burdens are heavy, or your issues are too much for you to deal with, God's word gives assurance of his presence and power. Therefore, I invite you to turn to the source of your power and turn to the word of God.

Despite the heaviness of your burdens, the depth of your valleys, the height of your mountains or staggering effect of life's unexpected twists and turns, God's word removes the doubt that takes control of our former positive outlook. His word gives us assurance that we are not forsaken, denied or forgotten. That is a word each one of us needs to take hold. The knowledge that we are truly covered on all sides gives us confidence to move forward. God's word can help us through our toughest times and help us overcome many of the uncertain, catastrophic experiences life continues to present to us.

The Power: Building, Walking, Living Your Faith

Part II – Walking, Living Your Faith

The most important step we must take on our faith journey is walking and living faith. The Bible tells us in James 2:17-18, "So faith by itself, if it has no works, is dead. But someone will say, "You have faith and I have works." Show me your faith apart from your works, and I by my works will show you my faith." In other words, talking faith is okay. It means we are focused on the realization of God. It indicates we give God the respect of who He is and what He is. Talking faith is also a tool that describes who we are, to an extent. It can impress others to believe that we are truly committed to God and God's way. But, often, talking faith can be nothing more than a side show. Listen to what the Bible says, "Faith without works is dead." If all we have is the talk, we don't have very much. Some have said that talk is cheap. God wants to see our works, our faith in action. Just because we have gone through or are going through tumultuous trials of life, and it seems we are taking more than we can possibly bear—more sickness and disappointment, more lies, more rejection, deception, hurt, pains, broken hearts, despair, grief, darkness, loneliness and sadness, more and more of the worst life has to offer—we must have enough faith in God to believe that he will provide a way out of no way for us.

You may not see it. Perhaps you have been told that nothing can be done for you, or no one whom you have called on for help has responded in a positive way. Every direction taken turns you around to another dead end. The problem? Trouble gets worse by the seconds, and your options in hope of setting things right seem to have been exhausted.

Instead of doing what sounds easy and giving up, throwing in the towel or quitting, avoiding more pains and frustrations, fall back on your faith in God, believe without a doubt that God is about to help you overcome the certain defeat, which the world has claimed for you. It is during times like this that you must live and walk your faith. Hebrews 11:1 says, "Now faith is the substance of things hoped for, the evidence of things not seen. What this is saying to us is that when we don't have anything else, we must have faith in God. I can't see it, but I can envision it. I can't see it, but I can feel it in my mind.

Just as Abel had faith and offered God a more excellent sacrifice than Cain, or as Enoch's faith led him to the kingdom so he would not see death, or as Sara, who had faith that she would conceive a child past her child-bearing years, we, too, must have unwavering faith in God. With this faith we can move forward. We can win at the games of life. Most importantly, we can go all the way.

Nothing can stop you when you have total commitment to God and unwavering faith in God.

Doubt

Doubt will make you question God's word and whether or not the good promises of God are really real. By faith, doubt can't stop us.

Discouragement

The words of others, the negative news, and the "he-say", "she-say", "they-say" reports, will have you focusing on your problems rather than on God. By faith, discouragement can't stop us!

Diversion

Diversion will make the wrong things seem attractive so that we detour from the path and settle for less than God's promises. By faith, diversion can't stop us!

Defeat

Defeat is an evil of the world that will tell you, you are a failure, so that you don't even try to pursue God's favor and promises. By faith, defeat can't stop us!

Delay

Either you procrastinate pursuing what God has birthed in you, or the lack of endurance to get to the promise causes you to get discouraged. By faith delay can't stop us!

Why? Because with true faith in God we know that just because the promise is delayed does not mean it is denied. Strong, true faith lifts us and helps us run faster to conquer what God has in store for us. True faith in God will never let us down.

Being put down, brought down, turned down, and let down because of persecution, will never stop us again. Therefore, rise up, put on your wings and get ready to fly high like the eagle God intended you to be.

Looking Inside and Living Again

What new insights did you gain about yourself? About God?

_____

_____

_____

_____

_____

_____

_____

How can God use you during your time of struggle?

_____

_____

_____

_____

_____

_____

_____

What is your plan of action for triumph today?

_____

_____

_____

_____

_____

_____

_____

"Not in Vain"

Mrs. Janice Anderson Hayes

In His infinite wisdom, God shows us the way
To find life everlasting as we journey day-by-day.

We need only to listen and stay steadfast in His word.
We must pray without ceasing as He guides and
undergirds.

But staying the course and keeping the faith,
Is a task tried and true in not going astray.

For the enemy is seeking whom he may devour,
And targets children of the King every minute, every hour.

He works through the weak and those who backslide,
Using them to inflict hatred, torment and lies.

They are his instruments of persecution and pain,
With their falsehoods, deception and attempts to defame.

Then he brings hurt through death and disease,
And financial woes and vices, he uses with ease.

He creeps in through sickness of spirit, body, heart, mind
and soul,
To attack God's faithful and to loosen their hold.

Oh, the struggle is real in our quest to do right,
And though battle-scarred and wounded, we can't give up
the fight

Perhaps Satan's brought you anguish, temptation or sorrow,
And almost convinced you there's no hope for tomorrow.

But, remember nothing separates us from the love of God,
And nothing is mightier than His Holy Word!

So hold on, be strong, trust and obey,
And then watch God cover and keep you every day.

For the reward is GREAT – It is the crown of life.
God knows we've endured grief, heartache and strife.

No matter the hurt and no matter the pain,
Hold on my child – your struggle is not in vain!

Who Can You Trust?

This is a call for strength, courage and confidence for people who have gone through great tribulation in life; People who have faced the raging seas of life or been knocked down because of untrustworthy relationships. You must be careful, prayerful and watchful of all those who call you friend.

- True, godly people will stand with you through your good and bad.
- True friends won't forsake or betray you for personal gain or because of disagreement or even friction that comes between you.
- True friends work together to solve their differences.
- True friends remain closely and tightly knit together, regardless of the circumstances. That's why you must build a personal, permanent and intimate relationship with Jesus Christ.

No matter the situation or circumstance, Jesus sticks closer to us, than any brother or sister. This same Jesus will not forsake or deny us. Remember how he said in St. John 15:13, "No one has greater love than this, to lay down one's life for one's friends."

Your relationship with Jesus should be your top priority. You need to know that during your most menacing and trying times, someone is standing by you. Jesus provides us with a relationship that is built on a solid foundation.

Nothing negative said about you can break this relationship apart. No rumors or allegations can cut into it. No futile stares can change his mind or commitment to you. Jesus reminds us that even if we make mistakes or fall down, as one who sticks close to us, he will not only be there, but he will also help us get back up. He will restore us to an upright position.

Regardless of who you are, your status or position in the community, or even in the church, life can throw you a curve like nothing else can. It will make you feel lost and alone, like a sheep without a shepherd. You will feel empty, thinking no one cares for you, not even God. When you are feeling empty and alone it can make you lose your belief that things will work out. You can lose your desire to rise up and fight. You may even stop trying, thinking you can't overcome your heartaches, pains and troubles.

I want you to understand that the Devil loves it when you are in the "I can't" mode. I can't overcome, move forward or win. When all you deal with are the reasons why you can't do something, it only gives the Devil victory over your life. Your "I can't" thinking overshadows the will of God for you, which is an "I can" attitude. Always remember you are not the Devil's property. He didn't create you. Maybe he is responsible for your problems, troubles, sadness, and frustrations, but YOU? No way! He's not even your friend, so don't believe that you can trust him on anything. Secondly, he will use anything and anybody to get you, stop you, bring you down and hinder your forward progress. He will dim your outlook on life and leave you feeling totally deserted.

What we need to do is add it all up. The Devil's job description is to steal, kill and destroy us. While Jesus is trying to give life and desires us to have it more abundantly, he also is saying to you and me that he will stick to us closer than a brother. This is not a statement to take lightly. Even brothers who have been with you from birth can turn on you. But, Jesus never will.

In Genesis the 37th chapter we are given the amazing account of Joseph and his brothers. Joseph was one with great ambition who had dreams of how God would bless him. Joseph was Jacob's youngest son, born in Jacob's old age. Because of this he found favor with his father. His brothers already had uneasy feelings toward Joseph because of the relationship Joseph had with their father. They were even upset and had bitter feelings toward their baby brother.

People you thought you could trust and believe in will turn on you because of your favor, blessings, and goodness. Your outlook on life and sometimes anything positive that happens in your life fuels the fires of deceit. One of the worst things that can happen to you is having blind faith. Blind faith is like standing on shaky ground. You're hoping and praying that it holds up and won't give way at your most crucial point.

Joseph was only seventeen years old and believed family was important. He believed that brothers were special, and that regardless of what transpired they would always support each other. He believed because they were brothers they cared for, loved and had great affection toward one another. This is the understanding we, too, have had throughout our lifetime. However, we must learn to look beyond the rim and see things as they really are. Look again at this story. It was another person who caused the feelings of Joseph's brothers toward him to take an even bigger turn toward bitterness and hatred. Jacob, their father, gave Joseph a special gift—a beautiful robe with sleeves, also described as decorated. The Bible says in Genesis 37:4 that his brothers hated Joseph because of their father's partiality. His older, wiser brothers hated that Joseph received so much of Jacob's attention.

You will be disliked, and others will grow frustrated, and even at odds with you because of your popularity. This was evident by the behavior of Joseph's brothers, who despised him because of the relationship and the affection shown him by their father. Sadly, this was not the end of the events that dramatically changed Joseph's life.

Joseph was a dreamer who believed his dreams were a gift from God. He believed and trusted without a doubt, these dreams would come to fruition. The problem for Joseph was his inability to keep them to himself. Many of our dreams never make it pass the bed, sofa or chair where we dream them because of our fear that if shared with others, we may fall in disfavor, think ourselves better or more important than others, especially if our role in the dream is authoritative and strong. But, because we feel compelled to share these dreams full of life-like emotions and imagery, we easily evoke a self-image of greatness that can initiate feelings of confusion or even bitterness among others. Our own excitement about the realism of these dreams can even cause distance when those close to us are less than favorable and diminutive characters in those dreams.

Joseph was a victim of his own dreams. The Bible said in Genesis 37:5 that, "Once Joseph had a dream, and when he told it to his brothers, they hated him even more." Remember they already hated him because of their father's favor towards him. But, now Joseph dared to dream essentially that he was better than his brothers. Imagine the depth of disdain they had for Joseph. "You dare to dream that you are better than we are that you are something special, and that we will honor you." How human! Hatred personified!

Listen to the dream of Joseph beginning with Genesis 37:6.

> "He said to them, listen to the dream that I dreamed. [7] There we were binding sheaves in the field. Suddenly my sheaf rose and stood upright; then your sheaves gathered around it, and bowed down to my sheaf." 8 His brothers said to him,

"Are you indeed to reign over us? Are you indeed to have dominion over us?" So they hated him even more because of his dreams and his words."

Shouldn't you be able to tell those, whom you love, trust and believe in, the truth, without retaliation? Shouldn't you be able to share your deepest thoughts, those things on your heart, with those whom you have lived, walked, grown up with, cared for and protected? Shouldn't you be able to trust them? But, sharing the truth can be dangerous. It is sad that this young seventeen-year-old young man couldn't trust his own brothers enough to tell them what God was about to do for him. Then who can you trust? If not your own families, church members and friends, those whom you have cared for and loved? Who, if not the friends you have counted on and who have counted on you?

It is true that your favor with God and with others can be your downfall. Your good intentions, hard work, loving kindness and unwavering faith can be your death sentence. Your desire to be more, do more, accomplish more, serve more, give more and grow more can cause the very ones whom you considered loved and cared for you, and who would never hurt, harm or betray you, to turn on you like a wild animal, determined to destroy you.

Well, it did not end for Joseph with the first dream, for he had another, and again it was so powerful he was compelled to share this magnificent dream.

27

Beginning with Genesis 37:9, it reads,

> He had another dream, and told
> it to his brothers, saying, "Look, I
> have had another dream: The
> sun, the moon, and eleven stars
> were bowing down to me." [10] But
> when he told it to his father and
> to his brothers, his father
> rebuked him, and said to him,
> "What kind of dream is this that
> you have had? Shall we indeed
> come, I and your mother and
> your brothers and bow to the
> ground before you?" [11] So his
> brothers were jealous of him, but
> his father kept the matter in
> mind.

   The hate of Joseph's brothers grew deeper, and they sought a way to get rid of him. The time came when Jacob wanted Joseph to go to Shechem and check on his brothers, who had been away for quite some time tending his flock. Joseph did as his father commanded and set out for Shechem, only to learn they had departed for Dothan, where he found them. But, when they saw Joseph approaching, they immediately put a plan into action. They stripped him of his decorated robe, took and threw him into a pit, hoping he would die there. But, when his brothers saw the Ishmaelites traveling from Gilead to Egypt, they decided instead of killing their own brother, they could just sell him, and never have to see him again. They followed through with the sale and soiled Joseph's coat with the blood of a goat to take to their father, under pretense that Joseph had been killed by a wild animal. Joseph was sold not once, but twice. First to the Midianites, who in turn sold Joseph in Egypt to Potiphar, one of Pharaoh's officials, who was the captain of the guard.

The kicker to this whole story is that Joseph learned he could not trust his own brothers, who allowed jealousy to control them and direct them down a path of deception and deceit. He could not trust the Midianites who sold him for profit to Pharaoh, who gave him to Potiphar. He could not trust Potiphar's wife who lied on him because she could not fulfill her wanton lust for him. He could not trust Potiphar, who had given him authority over many things in his household, for when Potiphar's wife lied on Joseph and accused him of having his way with her, Potiphar did not follow what was right or true. Instead, he accepted what his wife told him and threw Joseph into prison. Joseph was now an outcast, a so-called criminal. He was given a bad reputation, and labeled as everything but a child of God. He had no one to stand up for him, because of who had accused him of doing wrong. He could not trust the governing body, or even Pharaoh to do what was right. They had to protect and serve their own, and Joseph was nothing more than a servant; a nobody and a criminal. So, why would anyone stand up for him?

Although the list of those whom Joseph could not trust seemed endless, he found comfort in knowing there was one in whom he could always trust, and it was his God. Everything God had shown him and given him through his dreams became true. Although Joseph was in jail, God strengthened his power to interpret dreams. Neither Joseph nor the prisoners knew that the dreams he interpreted in prison would take him all the way to the palace of Pharaoh.

Two years past and Pharaoh began to have dreams that frustrated him because of their content and because he did not know their meaning. No one could help him interpret them. All of his magicians and "wise" men were baffled. Pharaoh soon learned about Joseph's great gift of interpretation from a member of Pharaoh's court who was a former prisoner jailed with Joseph. Intrigued with this information Pharaoh summoned Joseph to appear before him. What a surprise to Joseph. Not only was Pharaoh impressed with Joseph's ability to interpret the dreams, Pharaoh was overwhelmed with a proposal Joseph presented to handle the threat the dreams described, thus awarding Joseph a position as governor over the entire land.

Genesis 41:41 and following describes the events.

And Pharaoh said to Joseph, "See I
have set you over all the land of
Egypt. 43 He had him ride in the
chariot of his second-in-command;
and they cried out in front of him,
"Bow the knee". Thus he set him
over all the land of Egypt.

Later, because of great famine in Canaan, Joseph's
brothers came to Egypt seeking food. And, they bowed to
their brother just as Joseph had dreamed. As we read in
Genesis 43:26, "When Joseph came home, they brought
him the present that they had carried into the house, and
bowed to the ground before him."

Regardless of where you are in life or what has been
your past, you can truly take God at his word and trust
that he will never leave you or forsake you. This is the
word of God for the people of God. Thanks be to God.

Wake Up and Smell the Coffee
Scripture: St. Luke 22:1-6

The smell of coffee in the morning sends a message that may be interpreted as a reality we can count on, especially if it is a part of a morning ritual. It is the same each day. We wake up, smell it, and know it's time to do something. The day has begun.

As we journey through life we run into many opponents and stumbling blocks that try to hinder our forward progress. We are overwhelmed by the plots of those who desire our failure, our hurt and harm; those who want to see us totally destroyed. Some of this is done because those who are "bringing it on" think we can't handle it. Others want to see how you will respond and act after being hit hard with low body blows and the most powerful punches you can imagine. Our opponents want to see how we are going to match up. Like fighters, they think they know who we are and what they can expect of us. They already have a sense that we are going to act like they want us to act—like the ole folks would say—turn tail and run, or fight 'til our death; hate until we can't hate anymore; play dirty like our opponents; give up, give in or just plain throw in the towel.

One of the things they don't expect us to do is to stand and wait for God to show up and show out. They don't expect us to say,

- "I've been hurt by my opponent, but I'm going to stand."
- "I've been wounded, but I'm going to stand."
- "I've been talked about, put through hell and run down, but I'm going to stand."
- "I've been criticized and even humiliated, but I'm going to stand and wait for the Lord my God to show up with all power in his hand.

Here is the reason why. Just because the opponent doesn't fear the Lord doesn't mean I don't fear the Lord. Just because it was easy for them to lie on me in the face of God, doesn't mean that I don't believe in God's ability to examine their spirit and see the garbage that lies in them. Just because they can't see the good in me doesn't mean that God can't see the evil in them. That's why no matter the problem, situation or even the odds stacked up against you, you have to stand and wait for the Lord your God to demonstrate just who he is. Is there anybody here who believes that?

Now, here is the real problem. Most of the time those who try to hurt, harm and damage you are not your enemies. Rather, they are your so-called friends—those with whom you have broken bread, worshipped and praised God, celebrated with, cried, laughed, and prayed with. These are the ones who will turn on you like a common predator. Look at your neighbor and say, **"You better wake up and smell the coffee. The day has begun."**

- Everyone who pats you on the back does not think you're that great.
- All of those who smile in your face don't think you're special, gifted or all that.
- Everyone who says great and wonderful things about you cannot always be believed.
- All of those who say they love you and are your friends are the very ones who can't even stand to be around you.

Well, don't feel bad. Jesus had the same kind of people around him also. One of them was his close companion. He hung out with Jesus, ate with him, followed him, lifted him up publically with high regards; walked with him, talked with him and helped him in his ministry. His name was Judas.

Look at Judas. On one hand Jesus was the best thing that ever happened to him. He was giving Jesus high praises while calling him everything but who he was—the Most High God. On the other hand, he plotted to stab Jesus in the back.

Can you imagine that Judas, who was right there with Jesus, building him up, was at the same time tearing him down? This was the same man that claimed to love the Lord with all his heart. He would always greet him with Christian love and a holy kiss. The kiss showed affection and deep respect. It indicated a commitment to each other, to the ministry and to doing good to all God's people. It was a symbol of being on one accord. This kiss was also representative of a solid rock relationship that could not be destroyed under any circumstance. The kiss was a mantra, repeated over and over again—you are my Lord, my King and I will never deny you. The kiss was to Jesus and the disciples what secret handshakes, codes and signals are to sororities, fraternities and clubs which are not shared with just anyone. This kiss represented an eternal bond. But Judas betrayed the Lord with the most secret tribute—a kiss!

If someone can do such injustice to Jesus, who do you think you are that people won't touch or give you a kiss of betrayal? **You had better wake up and smell the coffee. The day has begun.**

Everybody doesn't want to see you make something of your life.

...see you crowned;

...see you lifted up higher than they are;

...see you smiling with a spirit of joy;

...want you to have peace of spirit, soul and mind;

...want you exuding confidence;

...living the life that God has ordained for you;

...shouting praises and giving God the highest glory;

...living in God's abundance;

...receiving God's favor.

You had better wake up and smell the coffee. The day has begun.

And, here's the kicker. When you wake up and smell the coffee, you learn to put all of your trust in God, and not in the "so calls". I don't mean you just put your trust in God; you put **ALL** your trust in God. **ALL** means nothing is left, divided or even shared. **ALL** means everything is surrendered and submitted to God because you trust in him. When you give God your **ALL**, watch how God starts turning things around in your life. Watch how God blesses you over, and over, and over. Watch how God takes care of you. Yes, the NEW day has begun.

Judas thought he would destroy Jesus when he betrayed him. He even believed Jesus could never rebound and would never have the power he once held. In his own twisted way he thought this was best for Jesus and the disciples. Judas tried to turn the tide. He believed this act would get Jesus to move, act and respond his way. Isn't it something that when people can't control you, can't force you to do what they want, they will turn on you and even betray the friendship, love, fellowship, common bond and even the commitment between you. That's why **you had better wake up and smell the coffee. The day has begun.**

- All good talk about you "ain't" good.
- All friendship "ain't" real.

- All relationships "ain't" everlasting.
- Some smiles are fake.
- Some pats on your back are not always meant with good intentions.
- Some compliments are not genuinely given and have ulterior motives.
- All affirmation is not intended to affirm, but to confirm a higher regard for the one applauding.
- Every statement made in confidence is not on a dead end street, but is instead like a runaway vehicle on an open highway. It will crash and so will you.

All kisses are not out of love and are not romantically intended to suggest commitment. The same people, who lift you up, sometimes will be the same ones who will try to tear you down with a kiss. **You had better wake up and smell the coffee knowing that everything that looks good to you "ain't" good for you.**

- Wake up and move forward.
- Wake up and claim your total prize.
- Wake up and not only climb that mountain, but take the mountain.
- Wake up and come out of the valley.
- Wake up and turn to God, not just for some things, but for **ALL** things.
- Wake up and move ahead knowing that God is with you everywhere you go. He is with you in your every challenge. He is with you no matter who or

what you face, how far you have to go or from where you have to come.

- Wake up and trust God for your going out and your coming in.
- Wake up and let him know, it's him in whom you love and believe.
- Wake up and smell the coffee of a new day that God is the one who has your back. He is the one that will cover you, carry you, hold you, and love you.

God is the one whom you can call and tell what you want, need, desire, and wish, knowing that he will come and supply not some but all of your needs and more than you could ever imagine.

Wake up and smell the coffee of a new day in God's love. Then you will know the smell and the taste of true love. Didn't you hear God's word saying, "Taste and see that the Lord is good?" He is good for your spirit, your mind, your heart and your future. Wake up and go!

- Go with the Lord all the way.
- Go with courage.
- Go with confidence.
- Go with power.
- Go with a mighty faith in God.
- Claim what he has for you in the name of God.

Wake up and smell a new opportunity!

Looking Inside and Living Again

What new insights did you gain about yourself? About God?

_____

_____

_____

_____

_____

_____

_____

How can God use you during your time of struggle?

_____

_____

_____

_____

_____

_____

_____

What is your plan of action for triumph today?

_____

_____

_____

_____

_____

_____

_____

It's More Than Going to Church

Jesus Christ gave us the Great Commission in St. Matthew 28:18 "And Jesus came and said to them, "All authority in heaven and on earth has been given to me. [19]Go therefore and make disciples of all nations, baptizing them in the name of the Father and of the Son and of the Holy Spirit."

God is telling us that the most important thing we can do is bring people to Christ, help them grow in their faith and become totally committed to him. We are to walk and talk to him daily. He is telling us to teach all people about his love and faithfulness to them, so they might learn to live a life of abundance. God's desire for us is good. He wants us living a healthy, happy and wealthy life—a life that brings us continuous peace and joy and strengthens us for our journey. He wants us to accomplish all of our goals for life, and to reach the top of the mountain as we live this life. God is expecting us to live life in the plus side, not the negative. In other words, God wants us to have our hearts desire. That's why it is so important that our lives are totally connected to him.

It's hard living a rewarding life if you don't know where or who your power source is. In St. Mark 4:35-41, it reads, "Tell us how Jesus rebuked the wind, and said peace! Be still! Then the wind ceased, and there was a dead calm. And, in verse 41 those who were aboard the ship said, "Who then is this that even the wind and the sea obey him?" If Jesus has the power to control the wind, rain and storms at sea, surely he can control the issues and circumstances in our lives.

That is why going to church is more than going to church. It should be the place where the disciples of Christ are teaching and encouraging others to become disciples. It should be the place where Christian love is exploding, where the people of God are supporting, loving and caring for each other. The picture of the church should be so crystal clear that others can easily see that it is the right place to be.

People should come running to the church realizing it is where they can meet, greet and be in relationship with not only other disciples, but Christ, the power source of our lives. St. Matthew 28:20 tells us that he is with us always. Jesus will always cover us, strengthen, encourage, lift up, help, bless and love each of us, and provide so much more to and for us. But to get to this point, the church must be more than a building or a name. It must be about the business of transforming "church folks" into disciples of Christ. He wants us to go into communities and turn them upside right, NOT upside down. He wants us busy working, teaching and encouraging people to come to him. But, hear this. We can't change anybody, lead anybody, assure or bring others to Christ unless we are trying to become like Christ ourselves.

Statistically it is said that more than 65% of the people we meet or talk to are not associated with any church, and more than 60% claim no religion. Some ask why it is people don't want to go to church. Why is it that more than 60% would rather be considered a NONE?

- A NONE than a Christian;
- A NONE than a disciple of Christ;
- A NONE than a child of God or a church member;
- A NONE than a believer or worshipper;
- A NONE than a committed saint of the Lord.

One reason is the way that the supposed-to-be-Christians, the children of God, act toward and treat one another.

- We talk down;
    - ...run down;
    - ...knock down;
    - ...bring down one another.
- We make false allegations and lie on one another.
- We act like a friend one minute and stab you in the back the next minute.
- We try to hurt and harm one another with wild rumors and, we use the most popular "I heard" or "they said" weapon.

Our conversation with a friend or someone else we know easily slips into an endless list of negative things about the pastor, the deacon, the trustee, the choir members, sister so-and-so or brother "you know who". We describe our version of what's wrong with the church.

We even share our list of the "who don't like me", "who I can't stand" and "who I don't like". Then, we turn around and invite them to come to church with us. They easily respond with an excuse about why they can't come. Then they start telling others what we said. I can hear the conversation going something like this:

> "Why would I want to go to church with them if that's what a church person, and a so-called Christian does? I'd rather not go. I would rather be a NONE, if that is what a Christian is supposed to be."

- Christians are supposed to build up one another not tear each other down.
- Christians are supposed to embrace one another, not reject one another.
- Christians are supposed to be lovers not haters.
- Christians are supposed to be motivators not down graders.
- Christians are supposed to be way makers not hinderers of the way.
- Christians are supposed to be bringing in the NONES, people who don't know the Lord, and have never met him, instead of running them away.
- Christians are supposed to be spreading the word of God, the good news of the gospel and not the negativity of the world.

Jesus Christ, our Lord and Savior did not let anything or anybody stop him from going into the world to make disciples. He went out seeking and saving the NONES. Jesus gave hope to the NONES. He gave them assurance that he would love them. He embraced them and most importantly, he showed them a new life. But, while Jesus was witnessing and encouraging the lost to come to him, and while he was trying to give them a new hope and outlook on life, the saints,

...the temple worshippers;

...the chief priests;

...the followers;

 ...the church people;

...the holy folks;

Talked about him;

...lied on him;

...spread rumors about him;

...ridiculed him;

...rejected and denied him;

And some of them even threw him under what we would call "the bus"!

He was persecuted for being one who loved, embraced, and cared for those who were down and out, weary, worn, tired and rejected by others. Even his home folks and those he prayed for and cared about ran him down.

They plotted against him, scandalized his name, and made false accusations against him. And some just blatantly lied on him for doing what was good and right.

Although negative drama was unfolding all around him, Jesus kept on going, teaching, preaching and loving. He kept on seeking, saving, encouraging and embracing the lost, the disenfranchised and the NONES. Despite being rejected by his hometown people, he did not stop! He was even ridiculously accused of being from Satan! However, **JESUS DID NOT STOP!**

As true disciples, we must have the same commitment and motivation as Jesus Christ our Lord and Savior. Instead of walking, running and turning away, we must go forth in confidence. Following the Great Commission of our King is the same charge given to us today as it was when Jesus gave it to his disciples. He said, "Go!" Go therefore into the world and make disciples. You can't stop or turn around because of ditches that have been dug for your failure, or mountains that have been orchestrated for you to unsuccessfully climb. The Lord is telling us to keep going, keep being positive and bringing the lost to him. Jesus has called us to claim and reclaim his people. He repeatedly says to us that the NONES are too important for us to abandon.

It is time for the people who say they are Christians, who say they love the Lord, who call themselves children of God, to start putting down those things that bring down the church. Consider this a 24/7 prescription for the cleansing step in our work of disciple-making:

- Put down gossiping.
- Put down jealousy.
- Put down unnecessary sensitivity.
- Put down backbiting.
- Put down pettiness.
- Put down scorekeeping about "who does what" in the church and how many times they do it.
- Put down hatred and envy.
- Put down cynicism and doubt.
- Put down whining.
- Put down worrying about the blessings of others.
- Put down thinking more of yourself than of others.
- Put down doing the minimum instead of striving for the best.
- Put down being less, causing stress and creating mess.
- Put down measuring how much favor another person receives.
- Put down twisting the truth just enough to seem believable.
- Put down blaming others and everything for your failures.

- Put down manipulation, aggravation, tribulation and degradation.

Once the cleansing process has begun and you are on a regular diet, add this lifelong prescription in the process–Jesus Christ!

- First thing in the morning after you wake up, take Jesus.
- With your morning coffee or tea, take Jesus.
- As you sit down for breakfast, have Jesus.
- Throughout your day, enjoy a steady dose of Jesus.
- In your meetings, conversations, breaks, lunches, dinners, and late night snacks, have Jesus.

It is time that we, the church, and the disciples of Christ, make Jesus the center of our lives and GO!

- GO and make disciples.
- GO live the abundant life that Christ has designated for us.
- GO and follow the example of Jesus' ministry.

But, understand that if you don't GO, nothing will happen, nothing will change, and all you will get is what you have already been getting. To GO means to move, to seek and to campaign by faith for what you know is to come. Disciples don't just come because we want them to come, and good things in our lives don't just happen. Going doesn't just bless others, it assures you that the favor, your blessings from God are truly coming. But, nothing can happen until you move.

- You want prosperity? GO after it!
- You want abundance? GO after it!
- You want happiness? GO after it!
- You want joy? GO after it!
- You want a new life? GO after it!
- You want peace? GO after it!
- You want love? GO after it!

Sitting and just talking about what you want, what you hope will take place, and what you hope will come your way, means nothing if you don't **MOVE** and **GO** after your desires. You want it, **GET UP and GO AFTER IT!** Look at the second portion of this commission: Make disciples of **ALL** people. God is not **ASKING** us to go and make disciples. No, God is **TELLING** us to **GO**. If God asks us, we would have a long laundry list of reasons **NOT** to **GO**!

- I don't feel like it.
- I've got something else to do.
- I'm tired.
- I'm busy.
- I'll do it tomorrow, next week or next month.
- Call me back and I'll give you my answer.

No, God is **TELLING** us to **GO**!

In other words, the Lord is expecting us to be used by him to transform the hearts and minds of people.

- He is expecting us to give them a new outlook and a new vision;
- He is expecting us to give them a new way of walking, talking and living;
- He is expecting us to give them a new belief, a new joy;
- He is expecting us to offer them Christ;
- He is expecting us to help edify the body of Christ by perfecting saints, for the work of the ministry, so that we will be unified in the faith and of the knowledge of the Son of God.

When we do this…When we do this, the whole church can truly say, "Amen".

Looking Inside and Living Again

What new insights did you gain about yourself? About God?

_____

_____

_____

_____

_____

_____

_____

How can God use you during your time of struggle?

_____

_____

_____

_____

_____

_____

_____

What is your plan of action for triumph today?

_____

_____

_____

_____

_____

_____

_____

"From Hysterical to Historical"
Scripture: Daniel 6:14-18

My brothers and sisters, some things in life can fight us so much that it sends us into places where we feel more than uneasy, more than scared, more than being unstable, more than just being worried to the point that it's frightening.

- Our eyes won't stop shedding tears.
- Our hearts won't stop racing at an uncontrollable pace.
- Our minds are at wits end.
- Our patience has run out.

We have become so desperate for something good to happen, it seems nothing can or will change our harrowing outcome.

- We could be sick and it looks as if we won't ever get any better.
- The bill collectors keep calling and it seems we will never catch up.
- Our love relationship is cracking so badly, not even a load of concrete can bring it back together.

We have had all manner of ungodly lies and false allegations spread from what seems like one end of the earth to the other and had your reputation turned upside down.

These things will rip your life apart, tear down all that you have built up and send you down a path of misery. Lies and false allegations can not only cause you to lose your standing in society, they can cost you your job, family, home, respect from others, a job promotion, an elected office in the community and a depletion of friends and family members. On top of this, when these kinds of attacks are perpetuated by those you know, and have supported and helped along the way, it will make you almost lose your mind. It will move you far from being down, depleted of joyfulness and peace, and will almost send you into a psychotic frenzy. Can you imagine hanging by a thin rope on the side of a cliff with nothing but rocks and other sharp objects beneath you, knowing that if the rope doesn't hold, death is imminent? That's why you must always have more trust,

> ...belief;

> ...understanding;

> ...faith; and

An intimate relationship with God.

This is why your commitment and faith in God does pay off. God will not leave you helpless to deal with all of the great challenges that you can face during this life. You can count on and trust God to stand with you, through the storms of life, the mighty seas that are trying to take you under, and the great winds that are trying to blow you away. He will stand with you, when the enemy stacks up against you, plots on you and tries, not only to hurt or harm you, but to take you out.

Look at the life of Daniel when King Nebuchadnezzar of Babylon came to Jerusalem and besieged it. They robed Jerusalem of the best and brightest young men; those who were without physical defects, handsome and versatile in every branch of wisdom who were also endowed with knowledge and insight, and competent to serve in the king's palace. They were taught the literature and language of the Chaldeans. They were educated for three years before being stationed in the king's court. Among them was Daniel who was faithful to the Lord.

Daniel totally trusted God for his going out and coming in. He trusted God for all good gifts that he would receive. Daniel was known to seek God's guidance on everything he did. He sought God to direct his path. He was also known as one who would pray to the Lord with ceremonious ritual. In other words, it wasn't just a quirk. It wasn't however and whenever. It wasn't happen stance or nonchalant. It wasn't only when everything was going his way. Daniel took time to pray every day—once in the morning, at mid-day and in the evening. He ceremoniously worshipped God with deliberate attention and intention. Although these times were set throughout the day, they were not the only times he prayed. His life was an ongoing conversation and consultation with God. It did not matter what else was going on, Daniel could be found praying at these times. His prayer life was such that these times belonged to God, and nothing else could deter him.

But now, Jerusalem had been conquered by the new king of Babylon, King Nebuchadnezzar. The Babylonians ransacked and robbed Jerusalem of its very best. They took the gold, silver, and the best of the three young Hebrew boys, whom they turned into slaves. However, Daniel found great favor from God, because of his faith and unwavering commitment to the Lord. Daniel was living the life that God desired for him. He was living on top of the world. Have you ever considered that the God we serve is the author of good success? Have I got a witness? God doesn't just want you to be successful, look successful, or act successful. He wants you to live good success, real success, and everlasting success. God wants you to overcome and rise above the handicaps, troubles, problems and "mountain/valley" experiences. God wants you to be all you can be. God wants you to be complete. But, do not be deceived into thinking that everyone wants the best for you. There are those who don't want you to be honored and recognized for what you do.

Everybody doesn't want to see the crown of victory on your head. Everybody doesn't want you living a healthy, happy and wealthy life, especially when they think they are more than you, better than you, and more equipped than you. Sometimes the reasons don't make any sense but they are still reasons to put you down and label you as inferior. They consider themselves more valuable to the world because they have more connections;

...more power;

...more knowledge;

...are more deserving;

MORE, MORE, MORE than you.
What they don't have is more favor from God than you may have. When you have God's favor, guess what? You have everything you need. I don't know about you, but I would rather have God's favor than all the silver and gold, than all the cattle on a thousand hills, than all the friends in the world. Why? Because, I believe with God's favor I have it all. My situation may look bleak. It may seem as though I am broken and in despair. I might not look, sound, act or live as if I have it all, but I do, because God's favor is enough to get me through;

...enough to help me to hold out just a little while longer;

...enough to turn my life upside right;

...enough to not only run this race, but to WIN this race. Have I got a witness?

Look at the situation with Daniel and how he moved up. Because he was liked by King Darius, the new king, who found favor in his sight, Daniel was now promoted with responsibility over the entire kingdom. He answered only to the King! Daniel was hated by the 120 satraps (officers), because of his favor with King Darius. However, Daniel's real favor was from God. While to have the King's favor was okay, God's favor was the exceptional prize.

The king's favor was temporary and God's favor was genuine.

The King's favor could be twisted and turned, and God's favor is non-negotiable.

Clearly, God's favor superseded King Darius' favor. If you have some doubt, check this out. When the others plotted against Daniel, agreeing their goal was to bring him down and cause him to lose the King's favor, nothing they tried worked. They sought to crush this foreigner who was running their country, giving orders and being recognized as the boss over everyone. Who is he that we should honor him?

Their plot was futile.

- Talking about it didn't work.
- Disliking Daniel didn't work.
- Calling him everything but a child of God didn't work.
- Accusing him with false allegations didn't work.
- Trying to ruin his reputation, his standing and his position didn't work.

So when they were running out of options, they decided to attack his practice of disciplined prayer, his relationship with his God. They knew Daniel wouldn't be able to turn away from his God. So, the plot thickened. They thought, "We got him now." They found an opening they could use to develop a tool of destruction.

The satraps relied on their ability to present Daniel as a lawbreaker. They created a document and gathered all the "haters" to sign it. All of those in powerful positions signed the document. The officers, satraps, counselors, prefects and governors agreed together that no one could call on another god, accept King Darius, for 30 days. Anyone who broke this law would suffer death in the lion's den. Oh, how proud they were of themselves. Picture them in the great hall laughing, high-fiving, and patting each other on the back for the great job they had done. My brothers and sisters it's a rugged road, a slippery slope, and a dangerous outcome when you mess with a child of God. You cannot win, so you might as well leave them alone.

Once the king signed the document, it was law and could not be changed, even if he wanted to change it. The designers of the document used a model of the Medes and the Persians which could not be revoked, not even by King Darius. He signed it as a gesture of goodness thinking Daniel was aware of and took part in its development. Once the document became official, they ran from post to post hanging the new law and making sure everyone saw it, especially Daniel. In addition to the narrow scope of the document, there were spies who watched Daniel day and night, knowing they would catch him in the act, sooner or later.

Well, they didn't have to wait very long. As Daniel read every word of the document, the enemy was satisfied that Daniel's demise was just a matter of time. But, Daniel was a devout worshipper.

- He didn't care because he trusted God.
- He wasn't worried, because he trusted God.
- He wasn't intimidated, because he trusted God.

Daniel rushed home in plain sight, got down on his knees and prayed to God. He prayed and praised God. He prayed and worshipped God. He sought God's mercy.

So, what did they do? They ran to the king shouting, "We caught him and there is no way around it. He must go to the lion's den. WE GOT HIM!" They continued describing the manner in which the plot unfolded joyfully shouting how Daniel read every word of the document as they watched from a distance. The satraps said to King Darius, "He showed total disrespect for you and prayed to his God anyway, despite the edict. To the lions he must go!"

Although the king was very distressed about the situation, he knew he could not do anything about it. He had signed the edict. It was law. So he gave the command and Daniel was seized and thrown into the den of lions. Can you imagine being cast in a den of hungry, ferocious, flesh-eating lions? Talk about hysterical and thinking that being a meal for the lions would be the worst way to die! Hysterical! Can you imagine the sound of hungry lions growling and fighting each other to see who would get the first bite of your fresh flesh! Daniel must have been thinking that he had met his end. There's no way out.

That is how we can feel when we are hysterical about a situation we don't think we can survive. It is worse than being scared with screaming, crying and gnashing of teeth.

It is far beyond shaking, trembling and cold sweats.

Hysterical situations create exceedingly great fear that leaves you ready to jump off a cliff. It can truly run you crazy. But instead of going off the deep end, Daniel turned to God. When you turn to God, you find strength to endure to the end. You find a way out of no way. You find joy in the midst of your sorrow and peace where there is confusion. Daniel could have just given up. But, he knew God was strong and mighty and would never fail him.

That night in the lion's den was fearful and frightening. It was horrifying. It could have been Daniel's night of death. Daniel was waiting. However, this long night of terror and fear was an example for us of how a hysterical scenario of tears and sorrow may come, but joy comes in the morning. In the morning the king ran to the den to see the outcome of Daniel's night of fright. "Daniel, Daniel", he cried. Daniel had to wake up and realize that he had gone from hysterical to the historical. Instead of being the meal ordered from a menu, the lions were Daniel's bed and covering.

- God can change your situation in the twinkling of an eye.
- God can bring you out of any tragedy.
- God can resurrect your dreams, your life and your outcome.

God can make the difference in any hysterical moment in your life. That's when you know all the hysteria and the drama becomes an historical account of God's promise of deliverance.

Persecuted for Righteousness Sake

Life itself presents plenty of challenges: Pain heartaches, problems, troubles, sickness, and the list continues. As we travel through life we are also faced with mountains we have to climb and overcome to reach the promises of blessings that God has in store for us. Life is already trying our patience and leading us from time to time on a roller coaster with many ups, downs, curves, twists and turns. At times, we are left feeling dizzy and a little confused. That is why it is so important that we focus on building a personal, permanent, intimate relationship with the Lord, Jesus Christ. This is important because the Lord desires nothing but good for us.

God wants you to have a life that rains down joy, peace and happiness. He wants you walking in the sunshine and not the torrential storms. He wants you feeling the comfort of his presence and to have the confidence of knowing that he is with you regardless of what you are dealing with or going through. This picture is perfectly clear. God wants you living a healthy, happy and prosperous life. He does not want you to suffer or go through one drought after another. He does not want you living in the valley, afraid to raise up your head. He does not want you to live like a sheep without a shepherd. You are his and his love for you is real, unwavering and everlasting. God rejoices when you live a good, Christian life that grants you his favor.

The problem is when the world recognizes that you are living a blessed life, surrounded by God's care and love, bitterness and hate of the world begins to manifest itself. Often you will find yourself under attack from all sides. These attacks can come from known enemies, which isn't a surprise. They can also come from those with whom you are in competition. This is no surprise either. Attacks can come from those who dislike or just plain don't care for you, or who don't want to see you get ahead in life or accomplish too much. Those who become jealous of what God is doing for you are determined to attack you. When you become too successful, too popular, or too blessed, your opponents despise you so much, they are anxious to tear you from your so-called "high horse" by any means necessary.

It is a shame that you cannot receive all that God wants you to have, without drawing complaints and bitterness from the enemies of the world. If you are surprised about being attacked, just think of how Jesus was treated. Think about all he had to endure. Jesus was born in Bethlehem, the City of David. He came to be our Lord and King, the Savior of the world, the one who forgives or sins. He came to make known his heavenly Father and to spread a message of repentance of sin. He gave sight to the blind and hearing to the deaf. He enabled the lame to walk. His touch made the unclean whole again. He even raised the dead to life and was called to be the Shepherd of the lost sheep. Jesus Christ came doing only good. He loved the unlovable and cared for the lonely and disenfranchised.

Jesus had compassion for all. He did not distinguish the difference between people because of race, physical size, condition, popularity, standing in society or reputation. He did not choose who to love based on education, background, neighborhood, family history or anything else that could be discriminating in determining his compassion and love for his neighbors. So, who were Jesus' neighbors? Were they the disciples, the temple worshippers, or the townspeople? Yes, and more than these persons, his neighbors were all who came in contact with him and sought a more personal, permanent, intimate, relationship with him.

The Gospel of St. Luke 19:1-10 tells us of a man named Zacchaeus who came to Jesus and had a life-changing experience. Jesus was passing through Jericho, where Zacchaeus lived and worked. He was a chief tax collector and was often accused of taking advantage of and cheating the people by over-charging them in their taxes. It was believed that the surplus or overpayment would stay in the pockets of the tax collectors. Zacchaeus benefited and had no consequences about the hardship he was placing on others. He thought about nothing but himself. The more he made the more he wanted, and he wasn't going to let anyone stand in his way. He had built a name throughout Jericho. It was not a good name. Instead, it was a name that none of us would want or like to have.

Zacchaeus was a scoundrel and a thief also known for his great wealth. He could vacation at the best and most expensive places. He could dine at all of the best restaurants and purchase whatever mode of transportation he wanted. He was revered with the best in society. One would consider Zacchaeus a person of means who lived a life of advantage. By every account he appeared happy and content with his life. But, as we look deeper, the truth reveals that Zacchaeus' life was not the picture of joy and contentment one might think. He was actually very sad and lonely. He had no true friends, no love or companionship. He had no peace with himself or his life. He saw himself as stagnant, going nowhere and without any real purpose or direction. He felt deserted and tormented by everyone he came in contact with. He was hollow and very miserable. He had cheated his way to the top, and found nothing there but loneliness and isolation. His wealth had come from hurting others, and he learned his riches could not buy the happiness he so longed to have. His much loved popularity wasn't worth having, for it was only empty admiration for his wealth and not for him. His ill-gotten gains won the popularity contest, and he was nothing more than the hated tax collector because of his cheating. The people of Jericho actually hated him. It is ironic that what he did drew him no favor among the people, but his rewards were coveted because he was skilled at his thievery.

Now, Zacchaeus heard about a man named Jesus, and of his love and compassion for all. He wanted to see who he was, but feared the attention from the crowd, for he was not cared for by them and was considered a sinner. However, Zacchaeus was determined, so he mustered up the strength and climbed a sycamore tree to make sure he wouldn't miss Jesus. Zacchaeus was small in stature and could have easily been lost in the crowd that was following Jesus. As Jesus passed by he recognized Zacchaeus in the tree and asked him to come down, for he would stay at his house. Before the stunned crowd, Zacchaeus came down and Jesus went home with him. Before the night concluded, this same man who cared only for himself promised to give half of his riches to the poor, and agreed to repay anyone he had cheated or defrauded, four times the amount he had taken. Jesus blessed him and assured him that same day he had received salvation.

Today, Jesus continues seeking and saving the lost. To paraphrase John Wesley, founder of Methodism, Jesus went about doing all the good he could, to all the people he could, and he hasn't stopped yet. As Christians, this type of lifestyle is not always embraced. Instead, you may gain nothing but rejection. It may be jealousy, envy or even hatred that you experience because you choose to follow Christ. And, although you are known for your goodness of heart, your commitment to Christ and your desire to do all you can for others, even those who say they know you, can turn against you. Jesus was persecuted for embracing Zacchaeus—a sinner!

This is what they did to Jesus! His persecution came in every way possible every day. He was talked about, rejected and ridiculed. They sought to dishonor him and ruin his reputation. This same man they followed and watched work miracles everyday became the target of betrayal. This Jesus brought healing to the sick, paralyzed and lame. He reached out to those with leprosy and took time to feed the masses of hungry people. He encouraged the weak and gave hope to the hopeless. Jesus instilled confidence in the down-trodden, and gave blessed assurance to those who felt defeated.

Rejection was not new to Jesus. His own hometown people of Nazareth turned against him. This was the place you would think supported Jesus and stood with him, if no one else did. They should have been the ones lifting him up and giving him the highest praise. Yet, they were on the other side, trying to destroy Jesus and bring him down. It disturbed Jesus so greatly that he remarked in St. Luke 4:24, "Truly I tell you no prophet is accepted in the prophet's hometown."

Consider your own life, and the very people you have blessed, or helped and lifted up from some traumatic drama. Think about all the ones you have reached out to and pulled up from disaster; those whom you guided and directed in everyday decision-making; the ones you prayed with, comforted in bereavement, and made sacrifices of personal finances, time and physical presence. It is important to repeat this description because of how easy it is for us to fall victim or get caught up in the hype. These are the ones expected to be your allies and stand strong against your enemies, only to learn that the enemy has been with you all along. You will learn it may be easier to stand with the stranger than this one whom you have called friend.

Jesus endured betrayal of one of his closest companions. His name was Judas. Judas conferred with the chief priests and officers of the temple about how he might betray Jesus to them. Read St. Luke 22:47-48 for this account.

> "While he was still speaking,
> suddenly a crowd came, and the
> one called Judas, one of the
> twelve, was leading them. He
> approached Jesus to kiss him. 48
> but Jesus said to him, "Judas is it
> with a kiss that you are betraying
> the Son of Man?"

It is hard to imagine that Judas, one of the twelve, could do such a thing against Jesus. Deception is a deadly weapon and those who use it can easily be the ones you trust and think are your friends. In reality they are your most dangerous enemies. Take a look at the crowd that followed Jesus. They cheered, praised and admired him. They were in awe of his power and blessed by his miracles. Yet, when given the choice because of a Jewish custom, they shouted to have Barabbas, a known criminal of notorious character, released from prison, and to have Jesus take his place.

St. Matthew's account in chapter 27, verse 23 recounts the event. "Then he [Pilate] asked, "Why, what evil has he [Jesus] done?" They shouted all the more, "Let him be crucified.""

Here is the kicker. Judas, the shouting crowd, and many whom Jesus had helped, stood with the elders, priests and the fickle crowd, knowing that Jesus was innocent.

- They knew he had done nothing wrong.
- Knew he was being set up on trumped up charges.
- Knew he was going through all of this persecution because of his love and compassion for all people.

He was being persecuted for righteousness sake! Even Pilate, the Roman Governor, knew Jesus was innocent, but rather than release Jesus and do what was just, Pilate put the decision in the hands of the shouting crowd, in hopes of giving himself a way out. So, Pilate washed his hands of the matter.

Your journey through life will have many bumps in the road that may turn your world upside down. You may be persecuted in ways that seem there is no way to ever bounce back. I encourage you to hold firmly to God's unchanging hand and continue to run this race and endure to the end.

St. Mark 13:9-13 reaffirms this by saying,

> "As for yourselves, beware for they will hand you over to councils; and you will be beaten in synagogues; and you will stand before governors and kings because of me, as a testimony to them [10] And the good news must first be proclaimed to all nations, [11]when they bring you to trial and hand you over, do not worry before-hand about what you are to say; but say whatever is given you at that time, for it is not you who speak, but the Holy Spirit. [12]Brother will betray brother to death, and a father his child and children will rise against parents, and have them put to death; [13]and you will be hated by all because of my name. But the one who endures to the end will be saved."

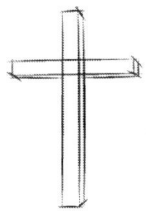

"Until God Signs Off"
Scripture: St. John 11:38-44

If you have been dwelling in the valley of life for a long time, and it seems that you will never come out of it, you cannot stop trying to climb out. If you're trying and trying to climb the mountain of life to reach your goals and claim your prize, and it seems like the more you climb, the higher the mountain is, don't give up. If it feels that you are going nowhere no matter how hard you try and you've become depressed and somewhat weary for the journey, regardless of how hard it has been, I stopped by to tell you, "Don't fret, don't throw in the towel, and just keep on moving toward the top. You have to understand the race isn't given to the swift, nor the battle to the strong, but to the one who endures to the end."

There was a man who had a great job, was respected at work and in the community. People were always saying very positive things about him. He was one of those persons who would help and support others. He was known for giving encouragement to the down-troddened and those going through the rough waves of life. He was friendly, even to those whom others considered as outcasts and nobody's, the lost and disenfranchised. This man was a giving person.

Yet, like this man, even when you go out of your way for others, trying to do good, and trying to show Christian compassion and love, others will try to attack you and destroy everything good that you are doing. This man was the victim of lies and allegations, and the people who were doing this were not strangers. They were his so-called friends, some of whom he had shown kindness. One of the things that people like the most is stuff that makes you look bad; they like the dirt and the ugly stuff of life that can tear a good person down.

You know we love the, "I heard", and the "they said." "Ain't" it something "they" always have something negative to say about somebody? The problem is who "they" are. Doesn't it frustrate you sometimes to hear "they" said this and "they" said that? Who are "they"? The world would be a whole lot better, without the "they-saiders". These so-called friends, his co-workers, lied and made false allegations against him costing him his job, his status in the community and his popularity. It stressed his family and ran away other co-workers from his presence. He was imprisoned without the physical walls and bars. Yet, people were running him down, laughing at him behind his back and making up false allegations about him. You know how it is when everybody wants to be a part of the party. Just look at the evening news and the way the dirt is shown. The greater the dirt, the better the mess, and the juicier the story.

They looked at this man and thought he had lost everything and knew he could never rise to the top again. Look at him. He had no job. He was burdened, weak, weary and worn.

He was tired, rejected by friends and co-workers and even some in the community who had at one time defended him, respected and accepted him. His situation looked and seemed hopeless. He was counted out by many who thought he would never rise up again.   Let me tell you something. I don't care how bad your situation looks or what type of nightmare you may be living, don't you quit, give up, give in or give out. Don't you stop, go back or turn around until **God** signs off!

Look at our text. Jesus had just gotten word that a person he loved and cared for was ill. Lazarus of Bethany, and his sisters Mary and Martha, were faithful followers of Jesus. It was Mary who anointed Jesus' feet with a very expensive ointment. She had bathed his feet with her tears and dried them with her hair. Jesus had forgiven her sins and she became devoted to him. It was Lazarus, her brother, who was very ill.

Doctors couldn't cure him, medicine couldn't heal him, and treatment and rest did him no good. So they sent word to Jesus telling him of Lazarus' condition, explaining that the situation didn't look good. Lazarus was growing weaker by the day and was fading fast. Mary and Martha were not only in a sad and sorrowful mood. They felt hopeless and helpless. They felt nothing could be done for their brother.

But when Jesus got word he didn't rush to the scene. He didn't drop everything else and come running as Mary and Martha expected. You know how we are when we are in need of Jesus. It doesn't matter what else is going on in the world. We expect him to show up immediately. Let me tell you something, it doesn't matter when Jesus shows up for your concerns. He will always be on time. He knows the timetable better than we do. He knows what has to be done to fix our situation or turn around our destiny. He knows how to get the job done. We just have to trust and believe in Him.

Mary and Martha's brother died, was funeralized and buried. The crowd was there tending the sisters and helping them deal with their sorrow, pain and grief. Several days later Jesus showed up. Lazarus had already been in the tomb for four days. When Martha heard Jesus had shown up, she went to meet him. Think about how you would be feeling. When you think someone you expected to be with you didn't come running when you called them; didn't drop what they were doing to come and see about you. According to St. John 11:21, Martha said to Jesus, "Lord, if you had been here, my brother would not have died." Martha had unwavering faith. She believed that no matter how bad it looked, how sick Lazarus had been, if Jesus had just shown up and spoken the word, Lazarus would still be alive and well. Then Martha said, "Yet, I know that whatever you ask him even now, he will give it to you." Jesus looked at her and said, "Your brother will rise again." Martha said to Him, "I know that he will rise again in the resurrection on the last day." But Jesus said to her, "I am the resurrection and the life. Those who believe in me, even though they die, will live."

In other words, Jesus was saying to Martha that death "ain't" death until I sign off.

As long as I'm with you, hold fast to your faith.

Hold fast to your beliefs that everything is going to work out for your good.

- Your valley will be filled.
- Your mountains will be climbed.
- Your walls will come down.
- Your closed doors will be opened.

Just hold on, I'm coming with power and favor. I'm coming with victory over all your opponents. I'm coming as a mighty warrior. Just you hold on.

Jesus looked at Mary and Martha and said, "Just show me where you laid him. Show me his grave." Sometimes all the Lord wants to see is the grave that others thought would be our burial place.

- Your grave of financial burdens;
- Your grave of sickness;
- Your grave of hardships;
- Your grave of unemployment;
- Your grave of torment;
- Your grave of lost love;
- Your grave of broken hearts;
- Your grave of misery and rejection;
- Your grave of rejection;

- Your grave of hopelessness;
- Your grave of loneliness;
- Your grave of poverty;
- Your grave of insecurity;
- Your grave of jealousy and envy;
- Your grave of self-pity and defeat.

Show me where you laid him. They said he had been there four days. Four days is nothing to Jesus. Some of us have been in some kind of grave all our lives. They said he smelled, his body was decaying and the bugs were probably feasting on him. Jesus said, "Just show me where you laid him."

Secondly, Jesus said, "Move the stone." Sometimes you can't get your blessing until the stone is moved;

> ...until you are uncovered;
> ...until you are free to press toward the mark of the higher calling;
> ...until you get all your junk out of your way;
> ...until you get a new attitude;
> ...until you get a new outlook;
> ...until you move the stones that are blocking the goodness of the Lord that is headed for you.

When they moved the stone, Martha said, "The smell, the stench is already coming forth." Some will think it is too late, because you look bad, smell bad. But Jesus said, "I told you that if you believe, you would see the glory of God. Jesus stood at the mouth of the tomb. The crowds looked on anxiously, waiting to see what was going to happen. Jesus shouted in a loud voice, "Lazarus come forth."

Lazarus came out walking stiff, his hands and feet bound with cloth, his face wrapped in cloth. He still looked as if he belonged in the grave. He smelled like the grave, and still acted like a dead person. But, he wasn't because Jesus hadn't signed off. Jesus looked at Lazarus walking bound, looking like he was still in the grave. Jesus told them to unbind Lazarus and let him go.

- Let go of all the things that are hindering your blessing from the Lord.
- Let go of your negativity.
- Let go of your doubting mind.
- Let go of all the things that keep you covered and cause you to look like the walking dead.

When Jesus saw Lazarus come out of the tomb still dressed as the dead, still moving like he was dead, Jesus said, "Loose him and let him go."

Lazarus couldn't be free, couldn't raise his hands to praise God, couldn't shout or tell anyone how good God had been, because he was still in his grave clothes. He was still wrapped up, tied up, and tangled up by those things that kept him down. He was no longer in the grave, but he still looked like he belonged there.

When Jesus raises you up, he wants you to come forth like something special–like the true child of God you are. When Jesus told them to loose Lazarus and let him go, he was saying to him, "I'm still with you." He was saying to Lazarus to get up and be all that you can be. I haven't signed off on your death. Rather, I've signed off on your prosperity, your abundance, your living a healthy, happy and wealthy life.

You may be counted out,

...washed up;

...rejected and dejected;

...disconnected, disassociated, disliked, discombobulated

And any other kind of "dis".

You may be hated, fired from your job, walked away from by your family and friends;

You may have been turned in, turned on, talked about, and lied on, forsaken and denied;

You may even be forgotten, buried and left for dead. But, I tell you today, that "don't" mean a thing unless God has signed off. Have I got a witness?

- Keep on talking.
- Keep on walking.
- Keep on moving forward.

- Keep on giving your best.
- Keep your head up, your mind focused and your goals in sight, until God signs off.

Tell the world they can't defeat you unless God signs off. Tell your hardships they can't break you, unless God signs off. Tell your troubles, headaches, pains, bitterness and hatred they can't overtake you unless God signs off. I stopped by to tell you today that God hasn't and will not sign off on you being defeated.

However, God has signed off on you overcoming the world. God has signed off on you reaching the top of the mountain. That's why you can say, "I'm still in this."

- You're still in this because God said so.
- You're still moving because God is with you.
- You're still in this because you can count on God.
- You're still in this because God is covering, embracing and holding you up.
- You're still in this because God has signed off on your victory sheet. He signed off on your faithfulness to him. He signed off so you would receive his favor, his abundance, his peace, his love, his mercy, his goodness, his everlasting joy.

And, because God signed off in your favor, you win!

78

Looking Inside and Living Again

What new insights did you gain about yourself? About God?

_____

_____

_____

_____

_____

_____

How can God use you during your time of struggle?

_____

_____

_____

_____

_____

_____

_____

What is your plan of action for triumph today?

_____

_____

_____

_____

_____

_____

_____

_____

The Victory Belongs to God

Sometimes while traveling through life we end up in places where we don't want to be. These are places that cause us to be at our worst, where nothing is enjoyable. We find nothing but a time of misery, pain, sorrow, grief and fear. It is a place where our bad gets worse and our worst turns into a nightmare. It's a place where we don't want to be. It's a place where everything we do goes wrong. Can you imagine living a life that is taking you on a downward, wild and terrifying spiral, with one crazy and frightening turn after another? No matter what you do, nothing seems to work and nothing goes your way. It's as if you are stuck in the quick sand of life and the harder you try to get out, the lower and faster you sink. Life at times can be almost unbearable.

This is the way it was in the biblical stories I now lift up to you.

When the disciples were on the boat with Jesus, to go to the other side of the sea, a great windstorm arose as never before. The wind was stronger than they had ever seen. The rain was pouring at an unbelievable pace. The waves were surging so high it appeared the boat would be overtaken. Those on board were experiencing raging fear, believing the boat was about to sink with them aboard.

The circumstances of life can cause us to lose hope, thinking there is no way out or around our impending doom. We feel the worst is going to overtake us.

Times like this cause a loss of confidence, loss of the will to press on, and loss of the strength to fight. This was the reality of the disciples on board the boat. Finally, when they looked for Jesus, he was asleep on a cushion in the stern.

Based on the knowledge the disciples had of Jesus and his power, it should have given them courage and confidence just knowing Jesus was on board with them. We should feel the same strength just knowing Jesus is on board in our lives today. Knowing this should cause us to breathe a sigh of relief. Knowing Jesus is on board should assure us that everything is going to be alright.

Knowing Jesus is on board should tell us that regardless of the present condition or forces that drive them, he is still in control. Look at St. Mark 4:39 and 40. "And he arose, and rebuked the wind, and said unto the sea, peace be still. And the wind ceased, and there was great calm. [40]And he said unto them, why are you so fearful? How is it that you have no faith?"

It is interesting that we say we know and trust in the Lord, yet we fail to turn our troubles, burdens and woes over to him to handle. When no one else can help, Jesus can fix the problem. Our challenge is to learn how to totally lean and depend on him. We miss our victories when we fail to surrender our cares and those things that frustrate or perplex us, over to the master problem-solver.

We try to determine the level of power available. We try to set parameters on Jesus by peeling off a problem or two the way we pull dollar bills from a tightly packed wallet. When we try to tackle everything ourselves, we find out there are too many problems to handle, and without Jesus, we simply cannot resolve the issues.

The disciples knew the storm was too overwhelming for them to manage. Without Jesus, this was going to turn into one of the greatest disasters in their lives. They believed this would be a watery grave with no survivors. But, once again, they witnessed the power of Jesus with this miracle at sea. They stood in great awe, and said one to another, "Who then is this, that even the wind and the sea obey him?" They realized this phenomenon was solely the work of Jesus. It was all Jesus. They just happened to be the beneficiaries of his marvelous works. They did nothing. They could do nothing. They simply received the reward—life! They were completely aware that this victory was from Jesus.

When a child of God is defeated, it is not just his or her defeat. It is a celebration for Satan and all of his sidekicks. This defeat represents rejoicing because it is perceived as a mighty blow against God. They want you to lose. They want you to be discouraged and distraught, thinking only of your miserable condition in life. In contrast, when you win and rise to the top, accomplishing everything God has ordained and intends for you to accomplish, **GOD GETS THE VICTORY!**

That is why no matter what your grief, hurts, pains, and sorrows are, or your suffering at being done wrong by the acts of others, your posture has to be a confident and courageous press forward, toward the mark of the higher calling in Christ Jesus. This is not a casual fight, a light gesture or a game to play when we are bored. This, my friends, is a real battle that requires real power. God is pushing for you and me in a serious battle against the world. Why? Well, if you lose, if I lose, give up, give in, throw in the towel and just quit, Satan and the gang rejoice. This becomes a significant win for them because, when they defeat us, and we represent God, they celebrate that God loses. However, when you keep going and endure to the end, you become blessed and God gets the victory.

Christians are soldiers in God's army. We are fighting, sacrificing and persevering for our Commander-in-Chief, the Mighty One, and the Great Deliverer. Our forward marching, our godly living and our warrior spirits glorify God. This act of faith and courage has been done before, by those who were not giants, not mighty in physical strength, not invincible, not royal kings and queens or engaged in the Armed Forces of this country. Instead, some were weak, struggling, outcasts, considered unworthy, less than, beneath and inferior to others.

But, all who trusted, believed in, stood for and with the Lord;

- All who trusted the Lord, not some of the way, but all the way;
- Those who had unwavering faith in God's power, mercy, and great love;
- Those who would not quit despite their circumstances;
- Those who fought against the fear of the challenge;
- Those who were determined to stay and stand strong on the word of God, came through history on nothing but the shoulders of God. In each case, they made it, but God "got" the victory!

Jericho was a mighty city and shut up from within and without where no one went out and no one came therein. But, by following God's command and walking around the city one time each day for six days, and seven times on the seventh day, the Lord gave them the city. The walls fell flat and the victory belonged to God.

In II Kings 8, we learn that even when a great famine hits your life and you lose everything, just trust God for restoration. Believe that he can give you back more than you ever lost. The Shunamite woman lost her son, her house and her land. But, instead of disbelief in God, her belief became stronger, with more conviction and lasting faith. Her son was raised from the dead and all she had lost was restored. The victory belonged to God.

Hezekiah was on his death bed and received the word from the Lord to set his house and affairs in order for he was surely going to die. But instead of totally giving up,

Hezekiah turned away from the world, away from all he knew and turned his face to the wall where it would be no one but him and the Lord. He cried, pleaded and prayed and the Lord gave him 15 more years of life.

Think about Job and how the Devil whipped him up one side and down the other side. Job had been one of the most blessed people you would ever know. He was the richest person in the East. He had a wonderful, large family of seven sons and three daughters. He had a beautiful, supportive wife, and he was perfectly healthy in mind, body and spirit. He loved and trusted the Lord for everything. But, everything was taken from him, including his wealth and his children. His wife looked at him in such turmoil and told him to just curse God and die. That's all the Devil wanted from him. But, Job held fast to the Lord. He turned to the Lord and lifted up his eyes toward heaven and blessed the Lord. Because of his faithfulness, Job's fortune and health was restored. God even blessed him with seven more sons and three more daughters. Because of his faithfulness, Job made it and God got the victory.

Therefore, don't cry over your hurts and pains.

- Don't cry over past, failed opportunities.
- Don't cry over what didn't go right yesterday.
- Don't cry over being done wrong in the past.
- Don't cry over what you've lost.

Instead of crying, press forward toward the victory and deliverance that comes your way. Take a look at the history of our deliverance.

- We have wandered in the desert.
- We have been thrown into a fiery furnace.
- We have stood in the lion's den.
- We have been swallowed up by the whale.
- We have been tossed in the boat on the raging sea.
- We have been beaten broken and downtrodden.
- We have been entangled in deceit.
- We have been cheated and manipulated.
- We have been sold into slavery like Joseph.
- We have been denied by our love ones.
- We have been betrayed by those whom we trusted.
- We have been abandoned by so-called faithful friends.
- We have been used;

    ...abused;

    ...smacked up;

    ...knocked down;

    ...and called everything but a child of God.

But each one of us has the opportunity of salvation, because of a love so deep, so great, so extreme, we could never understand it. That's why you can't give up, quit, stop, turn around or sit down as one who has no God. You can't sit and lose heart as one who has been defeated, or has no hope. You can't sit in the valley of despair as one who has no way out, has run out of options or who has nothing and no one in which to turn.

Don't you know that when you are standing on God's word, and when you are in a personal, permanent and intimate relationship with the Master, you know without a doubt that he will fight for you? He will be your mighty battle axe. He will be your way out of no way. When you lean and depend on him, he will deliver you.

When the world tells you that nothing else can be done just look at them and shout, "I don't serve a "nothing else" God. I serve a "something else" God."

- When your doctor tells you nothing else can be done about your situation;
- When your banker says nothing else can be done about your loan;
- When your mountain seems unmovable and it seems nothing else can be done, God is saying something else.

He is the "something else" God! Don't count God short and don't count him out. Don't think that just because it looks as if it's over, that it's over?

We serve and believe in a "something else" God. We serve a God who can give us victory in every one of our situations. It does not matter if everyone thinks your defeat is certain. That's what those who arrested Jesus Christ at the garden of Gethsemane thought.

- That's what Ananias, Caiaphas, the Pharisees and the Sanhedrin thought.
- That's what the Roman soldiers thought.
- That's what Judas thought.
- That's what Pontius Pilate thought.
- That's what Herod Antipas thought.
- That's what the crowd who shouted, "Crucify him" thought.

They thought Jesus was finished and nothing could be done for him. So, they treated him in the most vicious manner possible.

- He was denied even by those who called themselves his disciples.
- He was beaten.
- They spat on him, mocked him and did everything they could to disgrace him.
- They stripped him of his clothes and put a scarlet robe on him.
- They made a crown with 72 thorns that was too small, and pushed it down on his head.
- They made him carry his own cross up Mount Calvary, until he dropped it and needed help to carry it the rest of the way. They stretched him out wide and nailed his hands and feet to the cross.

But, they didn't stop there. With blood running down between the lock of his shoulders, a cruel Roman soldier took a spear and pierced Jesus in the side.

- Jesus hung on the cross until he died.
- They took his tortured and bruised body and laid it in a borrowed tomb. The chief priest, the elders, the Pharisees, Sadducees, Roman soldiers and Pontius Pilate, although he "washed' his hands of the matter, were celebrating.
- On Friday dark clouds covered the earth for three hours. The earth quaked as never before. The curtain secluding the holiest place in the temple was split apart from top to bottom. All this was on Friday.

Jesus took all of this to show us that even when you have gone through the worst of the worst, you cannot count yourself out. **AND IN NO WAY CAN YOU COUNT THE LORD OUT!**

We must realize that we are in it to win it. Look at what else happened to our Lord.

- His body was physically challenged.
- His holiness was challenged.
- His name was challenged.
- His teaching was challenged.
- His grace and mercy was challenged.
- His lordship as King of Kings was challenged.

- His love for us was challenged.
- His power was challenged.
- His purpose to save, redeem and give us eternal victory was challenged.

But when Sunday came, he rose from the grave with all power in his control.

On Sunday he was crowned the Mighty God, the Lord of Lords and the Prince of peace.

On Sunday he was crowned the Everlasting Father.

- Because he was victorious, we are winners.
- Because he was victorious, we are the benefactors.
- Because he was victorious, we receive the liberation from condemnation.

The point is this: Every time a child of God rises up after being down;

...bounces back after being considered defeated;

...makes a comeback after being assumed destroyed;

...comes out of the shells, caves and graves after being considered dead and even buried;

...we can celebrate!

But, the **VICTORY BELONGS TO GOD!**

Endure to the End
Scripture: Job 42:12-17

Ecclesiastes 9:11 says , "Again I saw that under the sun the race is not to the swift, nor the battle to the strong, nor bread to the wise, nor riches to the intelligent, nor favor to the skillful, but time and chance happen to them all. In addition, consider St. Mark 9:13b, "But the one who endures to the end will be saved." No matter what comes up in life, and how difficult our journeys are, never turn around, never give up and never give in. Keep going, fighting, praying, worshipping, and praising God and watch and see what the end will be.

There are times in our lives when we are hit by one crisis after another. At times they cause us to respond in such a way that we act as if we don't know who we are. We act like losers, like we are supposed to take one blow after another. When we lose our identity as one with courage and a will to move forward, or we lose our identity as a warrior in God's army, the world and others think they can take advantage of us. They will treat you like a chicken rather than the eagle that God has called us to be.

But, I tell you, you can't allow a crisis in your life to alter your course for success. You can't allow anyone else to determine your outcome. Your outcome is based on your ability and your courage to have unwavering faith in a God who can do all things. Take a look at this:

- When you trust God, he will smile on you.
- When you walk with God, he will order your steps.
- When you stand on God's word, he will fill you with wisdom.
- When you reach out to God, he will take your hand.
- When you believe God, he will knock down walls for you.
- When you put your faith in God, he will cover you.
- When you bless God's name, he will bless your going out and your coming in.
- When you know God, you don't know fear.
- When you know God, you don't have doubt.
- When you know God, you don't worry.
- When you know God, you don't lie.
- When you know God, you don't give up or give in.
- When you know God, you might fall down, get knocked down and get thrown down, but you will get up and fly again.
- When you know God, the Devil can't "whup" you, the world can't stop you, and your enemy can't defeat you, not so much because of who you are, but whose you are.

You have to believe that you are God's child, God's property, and he won't let anything or anybody defeat you. That's why no matter what you have been through or are going through, you have to give God the glory and still praise his name. God is still God, through your good and your bad. Acknowledge him and demonstrate your trust and faith in him, even when it seems all your hope is gone. Watch God's deliverance unfold before your very eyes.

- Praise God when you are hurting.
- Praise God when you are lost or frustrated.
- Praise God when you are going through the worst storm of your life.
- Praise God when everyone is against you.
- Praise God in gratefulness for all he has done in your life.
- Praise God as he takes you in whatever condition you are in and shapes you into a new creature.

As we look at our text we see how God blessed Job, how God took good care of his servant and how God showed this righteous man so much favor. In order to understand God's unconditional love for Job, we must start at the beginning where the calamities of Job's life began. We further need to understand the commitment and the endurance of Job. How could he have endured so much suffering?

The Bible plainly reveals to us that Job was first, faithful and true to God. Job loved the Lord with all his heart, soul and mind. Job's entire being belonged to God. He put God first in his life, and there was no compromise. Secondly, Job tried to do right and live his life for and with the Lord. Understand Job was no extraordinary person. Job had no invincible powers, he didn't rule any army, nor was he a miracle-worker with the ability to heal sickness or any other maladies. Job was just an ordinary man. But, he had extraordinary faith. The good news is God still uses ordinary people—men, women, boys and girls—just like me. As a matter of fact, if you let him, God can and will use YOU too!

- God uses the least to bring about the best.
- God uses a vessel to hold the uncontainable.
- God's mystery is overwhelming.
- God's astonishing acts are baffling.

God's decision to use ordinary people to do the extraordinary is so like God. God uses those who are willing to do God's will; people who will give their all, no matter the size their all might be. Job was just an ordinary person who was willing to do God's will. He wasn't immune to pain or financial distress, or even suffering. Job was just a man who loved the Lord.

Let's look briefly at what happed to Job. In chapters one and two, we see how Job trusted God even when his world tumbled down on him. The Bible tells us that Satan had been watching Job and had become frustrated because Job was so blessed by God. Don't you know the more God blesses you, shows you his favor and love, and bestows his abundant blessings upon you, Satan also becomes frustrated with you, and will do all he can to hinder your favor from the Lord.

The Bible said that Job was so blessed he was the richest man in the entire East. His substance was seven thousand sheep, three thousand camels, and five hundred yoke of oxen, five hundred donkeys and many servants. The Bible also said he had seven sons and three daughters. Just look at the reasons Job was blessed. He was also considered to be righteous and upright before the Lord.

When you, like Job, fear God and turn away from evil, God will take care of you. In other words, you can count on God. He is not like someone you thought you could count on, only to find out they were wolves in sheep's clothing, just waiting to attack and take you down. But, if you know the Lord, you have already experienced the real thing. This is the reason you need to have him on your side. He is the one you know is there for you when you can't count on, trust or depend on anyone else.

Job was upright and righteous. But, just because you are righteous, and have a heart for God, does not mean everything will always go your way. It doesn't mean trouble won't find you, or that you won't have any trials and tribulations. It does not mean you will be unencumbered by the strife and the cares of the world. However, it does mean that God will cover you when your troubles come. Have I got a witness?

Here was a man who lived a godly life, helped his neighbors, showed his brothers justice and mercy. But, he ran into hard times. Job, a man of God, a righteous and upright man, lost everything he had. The Bible said that when the servants of God presented themselves before the Lord, Satan also came and was among them.

"Ain't" that something? Satan won't even leave you alone in the house of the Lord. The Lord noticed Satan and asked him what he was doing there. Satan responded in his usual way, "Going up and down, to and fro in the earth seeking whom I may destroy". Listen well. Satan is out to destroy you. Satan is out to bring you down with heavy artillery. Satan is out to get YOU.

That day Satan was looking for somebody, so God asked him, as it is written in Job 1:8, "Have you considered my servant Job?" Now, understand this. God wasn't turning on Job. He wasn't giving Job over to Satan. God was actually bragging on Job. He knew Job. He trusted and believed in Job. He felt Job was true to his word, his faith and his love for Him. So, let me ask you a question. Can God brag on you? Can God trust that you will take whatever Satan brings into your life and still praise the name of the Lord? Are you willing to give up everything for the Lord, who gave up everything for you?

So God allowed Satan to touch Job's family and even take whatever he wanted from Job. But, God would not allow Satan to take Job's life. Here's something else you need to know about Satan. Because he loses one battle with you, because you don't give in right away, because you seem tougher than he expected, he WILL NOT STOP COMING AFTER YOU. He will even brag on you, tell you good things about yourself and will smile in your face, and pat you on the back. And, just when you think everything is on the up and up, he will hit you with a low blow, hoping to take you out, break your spirit, kill your joy, interrupt your peace, and make you stop believing in yourself and your God. Satan won't just come a little at a time. No, when it rains problems and troubles in your life, it pours, situation after situation, one after another.

Let's look at Job again. His sons and daughters were celebrating at the oldest son's house.

1. A messenger came unto Job, and told him the oxen were plowing and asses feeding beside them and Sabeans came and took them away, and killed all your servants except me.
2. While he was still speaking, another servant came and told him fire fell from heaven, burned up all your sheep, consumed all your servants except me.
3. While he was still speaking, another came and told Job the Chaldeans came, took all your camels and killed all your servants except me.

If this wasn't enough, if Job was not already reeling with grief, if Job was not already on the down slope of a roller coaster, if he was not already feeling rejected, sad, broken and tormented, just wait. There is more.

4. Another servant came and told Job his sons and daughters were killed, as a great wind came across the desert, struck the four corners of the house and fell on them.

It seemed that bad news just kept coming. When it rains, it pours. Job received so much bad news that you would think he would have been driven off the deep end. But instead, the Bible said in Job 1:20-21, [20]"Then Job arose, tore his robe, shaved his head, and fell on the ground and worshipped. [21]He said naked I came from my mother's womb, and naked shall I return there, the Lord gave and the Lord has taken away; blessed be the name of the Lord."

In the face of everything that Job was going through and had been through, he worshipped and praised the Lord.

In the midst of it all?	Worship!
...hardship, burdens?	Worship!
...loneliness?	Worship!
...financial depletion?	Worship!
...sickness?	Worship!
...bad news?	Worship!
...knocked down?	Worship!
...shut out?	Worship!
...stepped on?	Worship!
...talked about?	Worship!
...lied on?	Worship!
...persecuted?	Worship!

Worship and praise worked for Job. It brought him through, rescued him, renewed him and gave him new life. It will do the same thing for you.

- It will strengthen you to continue on.
- It will give you the power to endure when you're weak.
- It will give courage to stand the test.
- It will give you faith to endure to the end.

And, let me tell you something. This wasn't the end of the story. Satan was so furious because Job had been successful thus far. So, he went back to God and whined to God that this wasn't fair. You still have a fence around him. You're still covering him. You're still protecting him. So, Satan arrogantly challenged God and told him to take down the fence and allow him to touch Job's body. He told God he would make Job curse him to his face. I'll prove to you he is not that faithful. He's not that committed to you.

Satan was now coming straight after Job in full force. He had sores cover Job's body. Job was in so much pain, so much distress, so much agony, that his wife even told him to curse God and die. His friends came to visit him, looked at him and wouldn't say a word. Job looked bad with sores everywhere and pain he couldn't bear. Yet, Job stayed faithful to God. Job was committed to enduring, to see what the end would be.

The question I have for you today is, "Will you continue to worship God when you don't know how to pay your bills?"

"Will you trust God to comfort you when you are lonely and hurting?"

"Will you praise God with your time, your talent and your treasure when everything in your life is falling apart?"

"Will you follow God when your family walks away from you?"

"Will you be faithful to God when you are betrayed?

       ...stabbed in the back?

       ...persecuted?

       ...despised?

       ...used?

       ...abused?

       ...neglected?

       ...walked on?

       ...talked about?

       ...lied on?

Will you stay faithful? Can you endure? Will you endure?

When you endure to the end, God will bless you. If you don't believe me, look at what he did for Job:

God restored Job's fortune.

> ...restored his joy.

> ...restored his confidence.

> ...restored his outlook.

> ...restored his hope.

God gave Job twice as much as he ever had.

He now had 14,000 sheep

- 6,000 camels
- 1,000 yoke of oxen
- 1,000 donkeys

God restored Job's family again with seven sons and three daughters.

When you endure, just watch what God will do for you.

It's yours! Keep going!

It's yours! Don't you ever give up!

It's yours! Just ENDURE, whatever!

ENDURE to the end!

Looking Inside and Living Again

What new insights did you gain about yourself? About God?

_____

_____

_____

_____

_____

_____

_____

How can God use you during your time of struggle?

_____

_____

_____

_____

_____

_____

What is your plan of action for triumph today?

_____

_____

_____

_____

_____

_____

I'm Never Going Back There Again!

Scripture: II Samuel 9:7-13

A lot of things in life can cause us to be in great distress and can make us feel like we're living on the edge of night. At times it seems that we are living in the midst of a nightmare, where we are facing hardship from one avenue or another. It may be that we have been the victim of lies, false allegations, and rumors from the manufacturers of the "he said", "she said", "they said" stuff that has damaged your reputation, character and dreams for the future.

While some of us are either sick,

> ...broke,

> ...diseased,

> ...homeless,

> ...troubled,

> ...worried,

> ...depressed,

> ...deprived,

> ...discombobulated,

> ...disrespected,

> ...disconnected,

…or any other "dis" that you can think of, the others are wandering in the wilderness with no hope of finding the way out. We are just lost in **Lodebar**.

The Bible tells us that **Lodebar** is a barren land, where nothing is happening, nothing is going on. Everything is dead in **Lodeba**r. Who in their right mind wants to live in **Lodebar**? Excuse me while I correct myself. I don't mean **LIVE** because no one is living in **Lodeba**r. They only exist and barely survive.

Look at the definition of **Lodebar**—Barren land, nothing happening…everything dead.

- Everything is messed up.
- Everything is going or has gone wrong.
- When your back is up against the wall the arrows of all the wicked forces are aimed right at you and there seems to be no way around them.

That's Lodebar!

- When you try everything you can to get out of a bad situation…
- When you give it your very best to flip the script in your life…
- When you commit yourself, dedicate yourself to being positive and doing good but all your efforts continue to come up empty…

That's Lodebar!

When you make a mistake, do something wrong and you know it, and those you thought would always be there for you, and always have your back, turn on you...

That's Lodebar!

Think about how healthy, happy and wealthy you used to be. Now look at yourself. You're sick, sad and broke.

That's Lodebar!

You know what I'm talking about? It's when you answer your phone on the first ring not even noticing the number, but now you have to block all numbers and look carefully because of the bill collectors calling you.

That's Lodebar!

You used to go to the bank to withdraw money. It was just a matter of how much you wanted and in what denominations you needed. Now you have to check your balance to see if you can even go to the bank.

That's Lodebar!

You were feeling good all the time.

Now you're tired,

    ...sick,

    ...worried,

    ...depressed,

...stressed out,

...burned out,

...and almost put out.

That's Lodebar!

You used to live where everything was alive and well. Now you're living in the land where everything is dead or dying.

That's Lodebar!

You can't live in a land where everything is dead. Look at what happens to you in Lodebar.

- Your hope for a better life–dead!
- Your positive outlook for tomorrow–dead!
- Your vision of something good coming your way–dead!
- Your dreams of abundant living–dead!
- Being happy as you travel through this life–dead!
- Having unbelievable joy–dead!
- Having a peaceful life–dead!
- Having someone you can count on and depend on–dead!

S T O P!

"Ain't" no fun living in Lodebar. Look at your neighbor and say, "I'm tired of Lodebar."

As we examine our text, we see a great battle taking place between the Philistines and the Israelites, where Saul and his three sons were killed, including his son Jonathan, David's best and most trusted friend. It was the time that Israel fell in defeat and was conquered by the Philistines. David, upon hearing about the death of Saul and Jonathan, grieved greatly.

You see, Jonathan and David were not just friends. They were closer than brothers. As a matter of fact, they made a covenant that they would never leave one another and they would be faithful to each other's descendants as long as they lived. This covenant was made in blood as they cut their arms and put small rocks in the wounds so the mark would always be there, and they would never forget the covenant. It reminded them that their bond with each other was unbreakable.

Covenant means agreement. It means promise, everlasting, unending, unchangeable. Covenants are binding. And when you have a covenant, you have a special relationship. David and Jonathan's covenant wasn't just based on them. It went beyond the two of them and was a life covenant of commitment to each other's descendants. It was based on mutual trust.

You see a covenant has to be a trust relationship. Look at your neighbor, and say, "Trust!"

Both David and Jonathan trusted one another beyond life. In other words, their relationship was based on the fact that nothing could separate them from their covenant with each other. So after Saul and Jonathan were killed, and David was mourning their death, he looked at the scar on his arm and was immediately reminded of the covenant between them. David wanted to know if there was any of Jonathan's family left. There was a servant in the house named Ziba who used to serve Saul. David summoned Ziba and inquired about any remaining from Jonathan's family. He learned of a son named Mephibosheth. Following the death of Jonathan, there was a raid on the palace. As Ammiel, Mephibosheth's mother, tried to escape, she fell on him and his feet were crippled for life. They escaped to a barren land called Lodebar, where they were not known. In Lodebar they only found darkness and great despair.

This land was barren and bleak. There was nothing going on and nothing was happening. Mephibosheth a cripple, was broken, poor and in Lodebar, where nobody cared about him. He was treated like a nobody. He was talked down to, put down and knocked down because he had gone from being the son of a prince and the grandson of a king, to a nobody. He had lived in the palace among royalty. He was greeted each day with servants waiting on him, attending to all his needs. He rode in the grandest chariots, pulled by the finest horses. He associated with the who's who among the most important people. He dined at the tables that had been set for Kings.   He wore nothing but the finest of clothes and shoes. He was living high. There were no worries, no problems, no concerns, no hang-ups and no fears. He was living the life.

But, now this son of a prince and grandson of a king was living as a homeless person in Lodebar. Picture this. He is poor, dirty, smelly, cast out and knocked down by all. He had become a laughing stock. He had become the subject of all jokes. Just look at him.

He had lost the respect he used to have,

...lost his confidence,

...lost his peace,

...lost his joy,

...lost his heritage,

...lost his pride, his title, his authority, his name, his will to persevere, and his courage to stand and fight. He was lost in a lost place. He was lost in Lodebar. Yes, some of us today are lost in Lodebar.

But, when King David found out about Mephibosheth and the fact that he was living in Lodebar, David was concerned about him and knew that he had to go and rescue him. Don't you forget today that God is concerned about you. When you have small problems, major problems, tough problems and situations that you can't handle, don't forget that God is concerned about you!

When you are in covenant with the Lord;

When you are in agreement with the Lord;

When you know the Lord is in covenant with you, you know that God will be true to his word, when he says, "I will not fail you nor forsake you. I will not leave you and I will bless your coming in and your going out." Have I got a witness?

- Now, this is why God will do this. God understands covenant. He understands commitment. He understands faithfulness. God understands that when you are in covenant with someone, no matter where you are or what situation you are in, or how bad your troubles are;
- No matter how crippled, diseased, damaged, sad, lonely, broke, tired, weary, worn, rejected, dejected, oppressed or depressed you are;
- No matter if you feel like you are up the creek without a paddle, or on a raging sea in a boat that is sinking;
- No matter if you're in a fiery furnace or a lion's den, you can be sure that true covenant will find you, and will not rest until you are alright. Alright, alright! Have I got a witness?

That's why David could not rest when he heard about Mephibosheth. So David called his army together and went to Lodebar to find Mephibosheth.

But, like many of us, when God is trying to help us, when God is trying to bless us, when God is trying to do something magnificent in our lives, we do the same thing Mephibosheth did. We go into hiding because of our fears, our weaknesses, our grief, our sadness, hurts and frustrations; our sins, our wrongs and, because we are so terrified as to what is going to happen.

So Mephibosheth crawled under a table and hid from the soldiers of David, who were looking for him. Ain't no use in hiding from the Lord. The Lord has a covenant with you and he won't stop until he finds you.

So no matter if you feel like Mephibosheth living in Lodebar where nothing is going on in your life, nothing happening;

...where all around you is barren land, trouble on every side;

...where you're frustrated, worried, restless, tired, weary and worn;

...where you're feeling torn down;

...burdened down;

...put down;

...knocked down;

...broke down;

...shot down;

...kicked down;

...thrown down;

...or cut down, God will find you and God will send his angels to see about you. That's why, the songwriter said, "All night, all day, the angels keep watching over me." Don't you know that it is true even in **YOUR** Lodebar situation?

God has not and will not forsake you. God has not and will not leave you alone. God has not and will not leave you to deal with your Lodebar situation by yourself. Just as David sent his army to search for Mephibosheth, so God is sending his angels to search for you.

Good news! Good news! Good news!

The angels are on the way. I'm here to tell you. The angels are coming to save all of God's lost, disenfranchised, hurting, hopeless, down and out, rejected, scarred and scared people.

- He's coming to assure you that a better day is coming and another chance is here.
- New opportunities are on the horizon.
- A restoration is about to take place.
- Bowed down heads are about to be raised up.
- Broken hearts are about to be mended.
- Sad and sorrowful spirits are about to be replaced with joy, the kind that the world can't give you, and the world can't take away.
- Lost jobs are coming back.

- Depleted bank accounts are about to be replenished.
- Somebody's health is about to be restored.
- Somebody's problems are about to be solved.
- Somebody's life is about to be made whole.
- Somebody's future is about to be brighter.

So, look at this boy that David was looking for living in Lodebar. Look at him with people all around, mocking him, this Jewish prince on his crutches. I can see some of the men, as they would kick his crutches out from under his feet and laugh as he crashed to the filthy street. When they passed, the boy would pull himself up onto his crutches. Children would shout as he made his way slowly down the dirty street, "Here comes the King!" At first he would fight back. But over the years, his pride had been crushed, and his will so defeated that he wanted nothing more than to die in the howling wilderness.

But, David sent his royal guard to the wilderness to search for Mephibosheth. They looked everywhere in the house where he was supposed to be, but couldn't find him. Then one of the soldiers looked under the table and there he was, a downtrodden little man with his withered legs, pulled under him; his crude wooden crutches held tightly against his chest. He knew it was the end. But instead of reaching for their swords, the guard whom everyone knew when he came it meant someone was going to die, pulled the boy to his feet instead.

Stand up boy, the king wants to see you. Mephibosheth thought they just wanted to humiliate him before they killed him. They rode into the palace and hurried him before the King. He threw himself to the floor in his dirty rags, with nothing to offer to honor the king. And, there he cried out for mercy. David replied, "Don't be afraid. Mephibosheth didn't even wait for the king to finish. He bowed down and said, "What is your servant that you should notice a dead dog like me?" Check this out. He did not just say a dog, he said a dead dog. He was so defeated that he saw himself as one with no earthly worth.

So often when we have been down so long, hurting so long;

...we've been going nowhere too long;

...we've been running into one dead end after another for so long, we feel like we're living in a wilderness, a barren land, nothing growing, nothing producing. We feel like we are living in Lodebar, because Lodebar is where the downtrodden, negative talking, doubting, disbelievers live. In Lodebar, we feel like we can't help ourselves and no one else is there to help us.

We feel so hopeless, so down and out and so stuck to our perception that we know and expect nothing but the worst. Look at your neighbor and say, "I'm coming out of Lodebar, and never going back again!"

In Lodebar, we were talked about;

...lied on;

...accused of things we didn't do;

In Lodebar we were put down,

...brought down;

...and knocked down.

In Lodebar, our hopes and dreams faded away;

...our relationships went sour;

...our finances were depleted.

In Lodebar, our health dwindled;

...our outlook for brighter days turned dark;

...our opportunities to be all that God wanted us to be came to an end.

In Lodebar!

I'm never going back there again!

Let me tell you something.

- You can't let your past keep you in Lodebar.
- You can't let rumors and lies keep you in Lodebar.
- You can't let people who hate on you, keep you in Lodebar.
- You can't let your faults and failures, your past mistakes or your hang-ups keep you in Lodebar.

- You can't let the decisions of others,

   ...the negativity of others;

   ...the unforgiving spirits of others;

   ...the wicked ways of others;

   ...the plotting of others;

   ...the bitterness of others;

   ...the drama that others caused in your life, keep you in Lodebar!

But, God has a plan for your life and it is good. It is not in Lodebar!

- It's a plan of prosperity.
- It's a plan of abundance.
- Its' a plan of joy.
- Its' a plan of happiness.
- Its' a plan of peace.
- Its' a plan of comebacks.
- Its' a plan of enjoyment.
- Its' a plan of fulfillment.
- Its' a plan of favor.
- Its' a plan of true love.

WHY? Because he loves us so much!

He went to Calvary, to the cross. He was tortured with nails in his hands and feet, and a spear stuck in his side;

He bowed his head and died. He went to the grave, and endured all that he did for you and me, so we would never have to go to Lodebar again. And here's the kicker—when everybody thought it was over, done, complete and finished, three days later, he got up! Because he got up, we can be confident, assured and extremely certain, that no problems can hold us.

- Bad situations can't conquer us;
- High mountains can't overwhelm us;
- Low valleys can't control us;
- Satan's army can't defeat us.
- All the evil forces and powers of this world can't stop us.

So come out from under the table and be rescued from your Lodebar, and never, never, ever go back there again! For the Bible says: "Nothing can separate us from the love of Jesus Christ." No hardships;

...no distress;

..no persecution;

...no famine;

...no nakedness;

...no peril;

...not even the sword.

'For I am convinced that neither death, nor life, nor angels nor rulers nor things present, nor things to come, nor powers, nor heights, nor depths, nor anything else in all creation will be able to separate us from the love of God."

Come on out from under the table and be rescued from your Lodebar, and never go there again!

Looking Inside and Living Again

What new insights did you gain about yourself? About God?

_____
_____
_____
_____
_____
_____
_____

How can God use you during your time of struggle?

_____
_____
_____
_____
_____
_____
_____

What is your plan of action for triumph today?

_____
_____
_____
_____
_____
_____
_____

Poem - "I'm Striving"

I looked in the mirror and what did I see?

My enemy coming after me.

They hit me low with blows that were hard;

This they thought would separate me from my God.

But yet, I'm striving!

Although many tried to destroy my name,

And put me to an endless shame,

I never stopped, or quit, or gave up,

Because my God was ahead of their game

Yet, I'm still striving!

I'm never going to give up and this is oh so true,

No matter what people say, or what they do.

Because the Lord has said to me

This you can trust and you will see,

My love is real and lasts eternally.

So strive on my child,

Through all of the uncertainties of life

And this you remember, God will end all trouble and strife.

For the race is not given to the swift nor the strong,

But to the one who can keep striving on.

Through your storms and through your pain,
Even through your hurricanes,
Still strive on.
When there seems no end in sight,
And you feel no strength to fight,
Muster up what you can,
And God will help you win this race of life
You're in.
Just strive on to victory's end.
Strive on, my child! Strive on!